The Philosophy of Sartre

Continental European Philosophy

This series provides accessible and stimulating introductions to the ideas of continental thinkers who have shaped the fundamentals of European philosophical thought. Powerful and radical, the ideas of these philosophers have often been contested, but they remain key to understanding current philosophical thinking as well as the current direction of disciplines such as political science, literary theory, social theory, art history, and cultural studies. Each book seeks to combine clarity with depth, introducing fresh insights and wider perspectives while also providing a comprehensive survey of each thinker's philosophical ideas.

The Philosophy of Agamben
Catherine Mills

The Philosophy of Derrida
Mark Dooley and Liam Kavanagh

The Philosophy of Foucault
Todd May

The Philosophy of Gadamer
Jean Grondin

The Philosophy of Habermas
Andrew Edgar

The Philosophy of Heidegger
Michael Watts

The Philosophy of Hegel
Allen Speight

The Philosophy of Husserl
Burt C. Hopkins

The Philosophy of Kierkegaard
George Pattison

The Philosophy of Merleau-Ponty
Eric Matthews

The Philosophy of Nietzsche
Rex Welshon

The Philosophy of Sartre
Anthony Hatzimoysis

The Philosophy of Schopenhauer
Dale Jacquette

The Philosophy of Sartre

Anthony Hatzimoysis

McGill-Queen's University Press
Montreal & Kingston • Ithaca

ISBN 978-0-7735-3938-9 (cloth)
ISBN 978-0-7735-3939-6 (paper)

Legal deposit third quarter 2011
Bibliothèque nationale du Québec

Published simultaneously outside North America
by Acumen Publishing Limited

McGill-Queen's University Press acknowledges the financial support of the Government of Canada through the Canada Book Fund for its activities.

Library and Archives Canada Cataloguing in Publication

Hatzimoysis, Anthony
The philosophy of Sartre / Anthony Hatzimoysis.

(Continental European philosophy)
Includes bibliographical references and index.
ISBN 978-0-7735-3938-9 (bound).--ISBN 978-0-7735-3939-6 (pbk.)

1. Sartre, Jean-Paul, 1905-1980. 2. Existentialism. 3. Phenomenology.
I. Title. II. Series: Continental European philosophy

B2430.S34H38 2011 194 C2011-903195-7

Printed in the UK by MPG Books Group.

For Eva

Contents

Abbreviations

BN	*Being and Nothingness*
CDG	*Carnets de la drôle de guerre*: *Septembre 1939–Mars 1940*
EN	*L'Être et le néant: Essai d'ontologie phénoménologique*
ETE	*Esquisse d'une théorie des émotions*
IHP	"Intentionality: A Fundamental Idea in Husserl's Phenomenology"
Ion	*L'Imagination*
IPPI	*The Imaginary: A Phenomenological Psychology of the Imagination*
Ire	*L'Imaginaire: Psychologie phénoménologique de l'imagination*
LTE	*La Transcendance de l'Ego*
N	*Nausea*
OR	*Oeuvres Romanesque*
STE	*Sketch for a Theory of the Emotions*
TE	*The Transcendence of the Ego*

Preface

Jean-Paul Sartre is one of the most famous philosophers of recent times; he is also one of the most difficult. His fame owes much to his political and emotional engagements, as well as to the wealth of ideas expressed in his novels, plays, journals and critical essays. The difficulties arise as soon as we ask about the reasons for endorsing those ideas. In order to achieve a proper understanding of his views, and the reasons that might support them, we need to look at that part of Sartre's work where he explicitly addresses their content, presuppositions and implications; in other words, we need to explore his philosophy.

The philosophical writings of Sartre span fifty years. During that period, Sartre articulated, developed and elaborated, in sometimes unpredictable ways, a number of seminal arguments on major topics of philosophical enquiry. The desire for securing a reliable compass through the sea of Sartrean volumes, diaries and still unpublished manuscripts might make one adopt a sideways approach to Sartre's philosophy. We might wish to introduce his philosophy by categorizing his work under fixed headings, such as "existentialism", "socialism" or "phenomenology". This is a justifiable way to proceed if we already know what those terms mean, and how they should apply to each Sartrean text that is taken to express those schools of thought. Another approach may introduce Sartre's trajectory as filling the intellectual gap between, say, certain Austrian and German philosophers, on the one hand, and certain French or American philosophers, on the other. Such an approach might be correct in some respects, but it remains distinctively unhelpful for anyone with insufficient grasp of the work of the philosophers under consideration.

For the purposes of this book, I have taken the rather less travelled path of introducing Sartre's thought by focusing just on specific parts of Sartre's own work. Some references to other philosophers are of course inescapable – especially for those who wish to enquire into the context of Sartre's work.

A valuable source of feedback on my work on Sartre comes from teaching, for nearly a decade now, upper-year undergraduate and postgraduate students, who make up the kind of audience to which the present book is primarily addressed. It is not uncommon for students who are acquainted with Sartre through textbook paraphrases of some of his most popular claims, to experience serious puzzlement when they turn to the original texts expecting to see a fixed set of existentialist slogans popping up on every page. What they find instead is a philosopher working in meticulous detail on some fundamental problems in metaphysics, epistemology, the philosophy of value, meaning, mind and action. Moreover, the Sartrean approach to practical issues is hard to justify or, even, to interpret correctly, if it is not seen from within the Sartrean perspective of reality in general. I have accordingly focused on certain themes whose discussion might help introduce the reader to the Sartrean way of thinking about reality. The themes of intentionality, perception, emotion, imagination, being, existence and essence are also topics of concern to contemporary philosophical enquiry. I have thus tried to articulate how the Sartrean approach may advance our understanding of the current debates surrounding those issues. My reasoning, to be sure, is not that these are the only issues worth exploring in Sartre's voluminous output; it is rather that an exploration of several other topics presupposes or, at least, can most securely proceed on the back of a good grasp of the issues addressed in the present work.

One of the nice things about completing a manuscript is the opportunity it affords the author to acknowledge the help he received, mostly in the form of incisive remarks from several colleagues. I am first of all grateful to audiences in London, Oxford, Paris and St Petersburg, where some of the ideas presented in the book had their first airing. I should also thank Chris Daly, Peter Goldie, Harry Lesser and David Liggins for commenting astutely on parts of the manuscript.

I have debts of a different order to Steven Gerrard at Acumen for his Jobian patience, to John Shand for his valuable advice and to Jonathan Webber for his constructive remarks on the final draft.

Thanks are also due to the editors and publishers who kindly gave permission to use material from work that has previously appeared in print, including "The Philosopher and his Novel" (2003), "The Case Against Unconscious Emotions" (2007) and "Emotions in Heidegger and Sartre" (2010).

I hope the reader will find enough, in my brief presentation of Sartre's views, that might be worth arguing for – or against.

CHAPTER ONE

A narrative prelude

I

Sartre enters the systematic study of philosophy with an array of views that will affect the initial choice of themes to explore, and delineate some of the core theses he will later develop. Prominent among those views is that existence is irreducible to thought: the world is not the creation of a web of ideas, and depends for its existence on no design, human or divine. As such, all entities are "contingent", since they form part of a reality that exists without necessity or reason, and "gratuitous", as they lack justification, and serve no purpose: they simply are.

Often stated in an aphoristic manner, the above views are not self-evident. Yet their significance for appreciating Sartre's worldview is hard to overstate. They were first encountered on the pages of *La Nausée* (*Nausea*), a novel whose flowing narration of human experience imprints on the reader the material presence of things.[1] Written in the form of a personal diary, the novel gives us an intimate picture of events in the life of an individual whose thoughts and feelings are transformed as their objects start presenting themselves to his senses. The book is a rich source of ideas that, by Sartre's own standards, lacked at that stage the solidity required for a philosophical treatise.[2] It is these ideas, however, that will provide the rough material to Sartre's systematic argumentation: we thus need to grasp the former if we are to properly understand the latter.

The connection between perception and existence, and the relations between time and narrative, are just some of the issues the text invites us to explore. I shall delineate the main points expressed on each of those issues. I shall then briefly consider Sartre's own stance towards the philosophical views of his fictional hero.

II

Perception and understanding are often connected through the act of seeing: the hero of the novel, Antoine Roquentin, resolves to keep a diary "in order to see clearly".[3] Seeing is a sense that operates at a distance from its objects. The space between the perceiver and the item perceived accounts in part for a subject's awareness of being different from the object. That difference is an aspect of the subject's own sense of individuality, and is accompanied by awareness of the distinctness of each of the objects on which his sight may focus. Distance, therefore, is crucial for the independence, individuality and distinctness involved in the phenomenon of human vision.

The sense of distance, however, also allows for questions to arise about the correctness of the beliefs we form in light of the information our sight provides. Such questions will enter Roquentin's mind through an ordinary incident: on a stroll to the beach, while children were playing ducks and drakes, Roquentin picks up a pebble to throw to the sea, suddenly stops, drops the pebble and walks away, as the children start laughing at his bewildered face. What happened inside him involved apparently the fusion of two sense modalities, sight and touch:

> There was something which I saw and which disgusted me, but I no longer know whether I was looking at the sea or at the pebble. It was a flat pebble, completely dry on one side, wet and muddy on the other. I held it by the edges, with my fingers apart to avoid getting them dirty. (*N* 10; *OR* 6)

Touch is the sense in which the distance between oneself and the objects is cancelled. It is often the most reassuring of our senses, as we use it to feel the texture, or trace the contours of an object, defining clearly the limits of its body. That sense of security, however, disappears if we feel that an ordinary object extends over its familiar territory, shedding off the ways in which it used to be handled. For Roquentin, ordinary objects lose their domestic character, gaining, for the first time, their presence. As he is on the point of coming into his room, he stops short because he feels in his hand a cold object attracting his attention "by means of a sort of personality. I opened my hand and looked: I was simply holding the doorknob" (*N* 13; *OR* 8).

III

If touch creates such uneasiness, the return to sight should restore the distance between oneself and the world, providing the means for identifying each separate thing and its qualities for what they are. Distinctness, as we noted, is an important characteristic of perceived objects, and its loss often implies a defect in our sight, or in the ability to focus visually or conceptually. Our use of words for identifying properties aspires to convey such a distinctness, guarding against vagueness in the description of the object. Vagueness generates problems for a discourse that employs terms for which there are no sharp boundaries of correct application. A pragmatic way of dealing with this problem is to err on the generous side in our use of predicates; this allows communication to continue by predicating of an object characteristics that are to a certain extent different from the properties the object appears to have.

Such an approach assumes that vagueness reflects a limitation in the ways human beings map the world in language and thought. Yet a lack of sharp distinctions might be more than an accident of how we think and talk: vagueness infuses the object itself – or so it is experienced by Roquentin as he looks from his table at the bartender in a blue shirt with mauve braces. The braces can hardly be seen against the shirt; they are obliterated, buried in the blue:

> but that is false modesty; in point of fact they won't allow themselves to be forgotten, they annoy me with their sheep-like stubbornness, as if, setting out to become purple, they had stopped somewhere on the way without giving up their pretensions. You feel like telling them: "Go on, become purple and let's hear no more about it". (*N* 34; *OR* 26)

The blue shirt stands out against a wall in the colour of chocolate; and that also brings nausea. Only by this time, he feels that he is the one inside the nausea, which is over there, on the wall.

Roquentin is in the middle of a crisis, but he is unable to understand its cause. He considers that some change in his thoughts has affected the way he sees the world. This explanation, however, rings false to his experience. We may have thoughts about our seeing and touching, but they are part of our reflection on how we see or touch, and we would hardly confuse them with seeing, or touching itself. We hear, smell, taste, see and touch objects, which exist "over there", independently of us. It is this direct feel of the external world that makes it hard for Roquentin to dismiss what the senses present to him, as a mere projection of his mind.

The alternative explanation seems at first no less problematic. Is it possible for objects themselves to suddenly change in ways we would find upsetting? To answer this question we should consider what is involved in the conception of an object. A physical object is something connected to other things in space and time, on the one hand, and to previous instances of that thing's own history, on the other. These connections are causal, and the idea of causality is related to, if not exhausted by, our sense of regularity. Our understanding of the causal activities of an object are, thus, closely related to our experience of how the object behaves regularly. Whatever grounds causal relations in the world, however, it cannot be our sense of how things regularly behave. Physical objects transcend our ways of thinking, talking or making predictions about them, and they can certainly betray our expectation about how they ought to function.

Still, it is not clear why such change in the objects could create anything more than a practical inconvenience. What can be so upsetting about the behaviour of objects? The answer is that the way objects present themselves to his senses make Roquentin understand what it means to exist.

IV

Existence is the most discrete of our concepts: thinking or stating of every single thing that surrounds us that it exists is not a practice in which we normally engage. However, it is not possible to refer to anything in the world without existence being somehow involved in our sentence. When we do talk about existence, it is often by way of placing things under various categories, say that a page is or belongs to the category of white objects, or that white is a quality of this page; but even when, as we read, we touch and look at the page, we are far from forming the thought that it exists. If we were asked what existence was, we could well reply that it was nothing extraordinary, just a notion that added itself to external objects without changing anything in what they are. The nausea felt by Roquentin has changed all this. Existence lost its docile appearance and revealed itself as the very stuff of reality; everything is steeped in existence.

In our ordinary dealings with objects, existence hides itself. Accordingly, the realization of existence undermines the sense of identity and difference that makes up the plurality of things perceived. The diversity of objects is but a thin covering of the overwhelming presence of existence. Sitting on a park bench, Roquentin tries to calculate distances, and count trees and compare their heights: he tries to give back to things their individuality. The attempt, though, backfires, as the only thing he can ascertain is how superfluous it all is: "We were a heap of existents inconvenienced, embarrassed by ourselves, we hadn't the slightest reason for being there" (*N* 184; *OR* 152).

What makes everything superfluous is the lack of a justification for existing. An existent cannot be justified by another existent for two reasons. First, the other existent would itself need to be justified by another existent, hence leading our attempt for justification to an infinite regress. Second, justification is a normative notion, concerning not the fact that something is the case but the reason why that is; trying to justify an existent by reference to other existents would simply increase the list of what exists and could not on its own generate a reason for why it does.

We might perhaps wish to account for the existence of an object, say a newspaper page, by presenting it as a structured set of properties, of white colour, rectangular shape, of 30cm width and 40cm length, and so on. However, "white", "rectangular", "centimetre" and so on do not exist:[4] none of our ideas, concepts or words belongs to the world of existents, and the attempt to reduce the latter to the former is doomed to failure. Colour, shape or size *on their own* do not exist; only an actual object, the rough page of the newspaper, which smells of ink and smudges my fingers, does. Roquentin brings these thoughts together in a paragraph that will resonate through the rest of Sartrean work: "The essential thing is contingency. I mean that, by definition, existence is not necessity. To exist is simply to be there; what exists appears, lets itself be encountered, but you can never deduce it" (*N* 188; *OR* 154).

V

The belief in the contingency of existence is formed through an intuition that is locked in the present. The perception of motion and, along with it, the awareness of time seem to vanish. If it is hard to see how motion could disappear from view, it suffices to think that what we see is not an object called "motion", but things that change in space through time. Movement implies a point of transition, an intermediary between the before and the after, a gap in the plenitude of being. But no such gap is visible. The stirring of the leaves on a branch does not mark a passage from what was to be (the potential) to what is (the actual); it is the constant renewal of existents (*N* 190; *OR* 157).[5]

Time reigns unique in the diary of Roquentin. The very form of a personal journal reflects how lived experience is framed by intervals, discontinuous events and unfilled pauses. This fragmentary picture, however, is undermined from within by the very act of writing about it. To recount one's life is to attempt to find order in place of contingency. In telling a story, one takes a point in time and turns it into a beginning, that is, something pregnant with possibilities towards the story's end. Narration is always more than a keeping of records. We live our life forwards but we narrate it backwards, in the sense that our understanding of things past is guided by their conduciveness to things present (*N* 60–63; *OR* 48–50).

In Roquentin's case the interrelations of the past to the present, and the projection of the latter to the future, have been short-circuited. Continuity in time has to be regained through a number of devices, none of which sounds appealing. On the one hand, there is the public past of the commemoration days, religious holidays, bronze statues and condescending looks of the bourgeois portraits, all hanging nicely in the Municipal Gallery. On the other hand, there is the private past explored in his projected treatise on Monsieur de Rollebon, a notorious marquis at the turn of the nineteenth century, whose adventurous life was full of political intrigues and the subject of tantalizing anecdotes. Having spent years collecting data, Roquentin will eventually abandon that project when he realizes that what attracted him to the marquis' life was its adventures, and the problem with adventures is that they do not exist, or, rather, that they can exist only as narrated (*N* 61, 138–40; *OR* 49, 113–14). A moment in life could be an instant of adventure within a plot that weaves that moment to its (fascinating) future. However, when one is turning into a dark alley, or walking into a noisy pub, the future is not there. If there is such a thing as a "feeling of adventure", it is not the sense of anything experienced, but the wish for having in the future a past worth talking about.

VI

The attempted separation of living from talking or reminiscing about living is another aspect of the sharp distinction between the present and past. Is it possible to resist such divisions in one's experience? Roquentin will propose an answer that implies a particular understanding of artistic creation. His proposed solution is to introduce a different time from that of lived experience through the writing of a novel. The fictional hero will thus become the author of a fictional text, opening the door for modernist readings of the novel as a closed system whose end (the commitment of creating a novel) is realized by the novel itself, like a melody, is characterized by an internal necessity that composes its different parts into a harmonious whole. Listening to a jazz song, Roquentin feels ashamed of his being, as he is absorbed by the force by which each note follows the previous notes. The song is beyond the contingency and arbitrariness of his life, but it does not exist: "if I were to get up, if I were to snatch that record from the turntable which is holding it and if I were to break it in two, I wouldn't reach it. It is beyond – … I can't even hear it, I hear sounds, vibrations in the air which unveil it". The jazz song does not exist "since it has nothing superfluous: it is all the rest which is superfluous in relation to it. It is" (*N* 248; *OR* 206).

Roquentin now claims that all he ever wanted was to be. Exploring the jargon that separates existence from being, Roquentin aspires to wash his life from the unbearable "sin of existing" (*N* 251; *OR* 209) by being the creator of something that is beyond this time, abstract, necessary and indestructible. Roquentin's life is thus "saved", and along with it his understanding of time, by annulling the lived present for the sake of an aestheticized eternity.

We might think that the above approach to art represents Sartre's own understanding of his activity as an author. Such an interpretation would draw considerably on the assumption that the Roquentin who is planning a novel is the alter ego of his author.[7] As Sartre brought Roquentin into existence, so the latter explicates on Sartre's behalf the meaning of his text. *Nausea* is thus read as concluding with the unambiguous moral that an artistic object, be it a melody or a novel, is a fortress against the tide of superfluity that characterizes human existence. Is it correct, though, to identify Roquentin with Sartre on these matters? There are at least two reasons for answering this question in the negative.

The first reason is quite general. It concerns Sartre's own view of the activity in which Roquentin appears to devote so much of his time, and which becomes the privileged medium for the creation of his artistic desires: keeping a diary. Reflecting on his work of that period, Sartre notes: "I was not interested in myself at all … I had a horror of personal diaries, and I was thinking that human beings are not made for seeing themselves, but for fixing their look always in front of them" in the world (*CDG* 175, my trans.).

The second, and most important reason for dissociating Sartre from Roquentin is internal to the novel itself. The immense fascination with the jazz song is expressed from early on in the vocabulary of escape: Roquentin is absorbed in a melody that lives in "another time" as the notes fill the cafe from "so far away" (*N* 37–8; *OR* 28–9). While the citizens of the provincial town look for an excuse for their existence in the ritualized past, Roquentin aspires through art to transcend time altogether. Not unlike all the petit bourgeois criticized in the novel, Roquentin is seeking a justification in something outside "this time in which the world has fallen" (*N* 37; *OR* 28). The novel Roquentin desires to write would shine slim and hard "as steel", with events succeeding one another through a "rigorous necessity" that pushes forth a well-rounded, continuous, whole (*N* 252; *OR* 210). Whatever such a novel might be, it does not sound anything like a text of internally frustrated plot and discontinuous structure: that master drawing of contingency that Sartre created with *Nausea*.

CHAPTER TWO

Intentionality

I

In "Intentionality", a short article written around 1934, Sartre puts forward the basic thesis of his philosophical outlook: all consciousness is consciousness of something.[1] This apparently innocuous claim will determine some crucial steps in Sartre's argumentation: it informs his theory of the self; it motivates a new way of thinking about emotions; it guides his analysis of imagination; and it grounds his understanding of human existence. In the next four chapters we shall explore each of these issues in its turn. But, first, we need to address something more basic: what exactly does that claim mean?

The claim that all consciousness is consciousness of something gives expression to the doctrine of intentionality, according to which all and only mental states are directed towards something: in thought, towards what is thought; in perception, to what is perceived; in desire, at what is desired. Intentionality is widely acknowledged as a central feature of our mental life. What is original with Sartre is not the endorsement of intentionality but his distinctive way of unpacking that doctrine. The distinctiveness of his approach comes out clearly in his analysis of perceptual experience. In perception the world is directly revealed to us. In looking at a tree, for instance, you do not look at the idea of a tree, or at a picture of a tree, or at some immaterial replica of a tree. You see, touch or climb on objects, not their images. You see a tree, to be sure, but you see it "just where it is: at the side of the road, in the midst of the dust, alone and writhing in the heat" (IHP 4).

The directness of our contact with reality does not entail some metaphysical fusion of consciousness with the world. The perceived object cannot enter inside consciousness because consciousness is not an object with an inside and an outside, but a movement of fleeing oneself towards the world (IHP 4). If, *per impossible*, we were to enter "inside" a consciousness, we would be seized by a whirlwind and thrown outside, next to the tree, in the street, "because consciousness has no 'inside'"(IHP 5). The consciousness of a tree is not some large thing that includes two smaller things, one called "consciousness" and the other "tree"; rather, it is an event whereby one thing is "presented to", or "given to", or "aimed at by" consciousness.[2]

Appealing to the ordinary perception of spatiotemporal objects is a good way of illustrating the Sartrean claim that *consciousness is necessarily consciousness of something that is other than consciousness itself* (see *TE* 16).[3] This claim qualifies the general doctrine of intentionality in a subtle yet crucial way. Its point is to exclude a rival view of intentionality according to which consciousness is bound to things internal to the mind. We may distinguish here between two versions of that view. According to the first, a conscious phenomenon is a relation between a subject that perceives (thinks, desires or wills) and an intra-mental object;[4] according to the second, conscious experience involves the direct apprehension, or "animation" of internal items – such as uninterpreted data, impressions or sensations – that might stand in for, or represent, external objects that can be thus only indirectly apprehended, if at all.[5] Both versions seem to afford, in principle, a complete account of intentionality in the absence of any contact with the world outside the human mind. And that is something that Sartre finds philosophically – and, at times, almost personally – offensive (IHP 5). The whole point of Sartre's initial involvement with the notion of intentionality is to see how this notion can deliver us from the stifling atmosphere of subjectivism, and lead us back on to the open field of human engagement with the world.

Sartre thinks of consciousness as being necessarily directed at something other than peculiarly mental stuff. Understanding how this view of intentionality permeates Sartre's account of perceptual and affective phenomena is the aim of this chapter. In order to achieve this aim we need to introduce some vocabulary that will help us depict more accurately the structure of perceptual experience.

II

Our intentional relation to the world is an opening to the phenomena. The study of phenomena as they present themselves in our experience is the subject matter of phenomenology. What phenomenology purports to offer is an understanding of what appears to us, to the extent that, and in the exact manner in which, it does. To achieve this aim, phenomenological analysis switches attention from objects to the acts of consciousness through which the objects are presented to us. Yet that switch does not remove objects from view. On the contrary, it helps to make all the more vivid the rich texture of reality, and the subtlety of conscious activities through which the manifold of our experience is synthesized into a meaningful whole.

Consider an ordinary case of perceiving a wooden box, like the one that lies at the top corner of my bookcase: what I can see from where I sit is two sides, each receding from view in a different direction, neither looking square, both occluding from view any of the other sides. What I perceive is not a brown trapezoid, but a square side of the brown box viewed from a specific angle. I am directly aware of an object with six sides, four of which are given to me as not visible. If I stand up and walk towards the bookcase I will see different aspects of the box, my visual intentions will be multiplied, and they will be joined by tactile, and even olfactory intentions if I raise my hands, grasp and open the box to let the scent of dead roses fill the study. During that time, what I perceive is not a disorderly sequence of trapezoids, surfaces and colours floating around in space, but a physical object: the self same mahogany box. To the great variety of my experiences corresponds the unity of the object intended by my consciousness.[6]

Throughout this episode, the object of my perception was the same: the box. However, in some sense, what I was seeing at one moment from the comfort of my chair was not the same as what I was seeing at another moment, when, standing up, I held the box in my hands. Different aspects of the object came into view, making the two experiences differ in their content. Let us consider more carefully what that difference consists in, starting with the notion of "aspect".

III

Talk of "aspect" is ambiguous; it can have what we might call "subjectivist" and "objectivist" interpretations. In the objectivist sense, an aspect belongs to the object-side of the perceptual relation. Thus, a perceptual intuition that aims at the facing aspects of the object is "filled", whereas an intuition that targets the currently non-visible aspects of the object is "empty". We may rephrase this by stating that in a filled intuition the aspect is that through which an object is presented to us (see e.g. *TE* 13–14). But this turn of phrase invites a subjectivist reading of "aspect" as something intermediary, through which the perception has to pass in order to reach the object. In a subjectivist sense, the aspect is something internal to consciousness, for example, a set of data with which consciousness creates the appearance of a three-dimensional object. The objectivist account sets the aspect as lying outside of and, in that sense, as *transcendent* to, consciousness; the subjectivist understands "aspect" as being internal to and, in that sense, *immanent* to, consciousness. Which of the two meanings of "aspect" is intended by Sartre?

In the works published during the 1930s, Sartre's analysis seems to trade on the ambiguity of the notion of aspect. In my opinion, that is not so much a matter of theoretical indecisiveness on Sartre's part as a lack of his considering the issue explicitly. A reason for such lack of detailed consideration is that Sartre employs the term as one of the translations of the German word *Abschattung*, a word that supposedly enjoyed a standard usage in the phenomenological tradition.[7] The word *Abschattung*, though, is itself subject to different interpretations, as testified by the fact that it has been variously rendered by Sartre – and his commentators – as *esquisse*, *profil*, *projection*, *facette* and *face* (see e.g. *TE* 13–14, 59–60; *Ion* 141–7; *IPPI* 8; *Iere* 18; cf. *BN* 5; *EN* 15). Each of these words offers an indication of what the term might mean, without, though, committing its referent to either side of the objective–subjective division.

The French word *esquisse* (meaning "sketch" or "outline") is a common translation of *Abschattung*, and is often taken to denote the part of the object perceived by an observer. However, a "sketch" cannot literally be part of something; it might present at most a rendering of that thing. And while the term "outline" might bring us closer to the side of objects, it can arise only as an abstraction from the object whose outline it is. The word "profile" can perhaps be taken to denote something found in the object itself, but we can equally talk about the profile of something by referring to the subjective impression the thing arises in us. A "projection" is amenable to a subjectivist reading (for which what we see is thought to be nothing but a mere projection of our images or ideas onto the world), and to an objectivist interpretation (according to which the object "sends out" – and thus "projects" – to us, parts of itself). Finally, the terms *facette* and *face* can point to what we "take in" by facing an object, as well as to the object itself in its alleged capacity of orientating itself toward the observer, so as to "face" her directly.[8]

It might be thought that lack of clear distinctions could be a virtue for a theory of perception that purports to overcome the traditional metaphysical divide between "the subjective" and "the objective". However, that is not Sartre's own agenda. For him, intentionality is significant because it denotes the connection between two items that are clearly distinct and irreducible to each other: consciousness, and what one is conscious *of*. It is this predilection for sharp and clean conceptual distinctions that cancels any mixture of perceptual consciousness (which is "clear and lucid", "as a strong wind") and the perceived world (marked by the "solidity" of things) (IHP 4–5; *TE* 9).[9]

I submit that the Sartrean view of consciousness lends weight to an objectivist interpretation of "aspect", and kindred notions, as referring to integral parts of the object itself, rather than to some subjective "data", or "sensations" that supposedly mediate our relation to things.[10] That interpretation is supported by Sartre's subsequent writings on how perception differs from other types of intentional activity (*IPPI* 8–10), and acquires an unambiguous expression in his major work on "phenomenological ontology":

> It is true that things give themselves in profile; that is, simply by appearances. And it is true that each appearance refers to other appearances [of that same object]. But each of them is already in itself a transcendent being, not a subjective material of impressions – a plenitude of being, not a lack – a presence, not an absence. (*BN* 17; *EN* 27)[11]

IV

Perception is a conscious act that intends its object always in a specific way: the object appears from a particular angle, or at a certain distance, showing itself in this or that particular manner. Although in the multitude of our perceptual experiences of some object, what is revealed to us in profiles is the self-same object, the particular way the object appears to us, at each moment, might differ according to the standpoint we occupy relative to that object.[12] The difference here can be identified as a difference in the *content* of the various experiences of the same object.

On the face of it, the term "content" points to an ordinary and indispensable dimension of our experience, and its employment should raise no philosophical eyebrows. However, the notion of "content" has been burdened with so much metaphysical baggage that in the opening lines of "Intentionality", Sartre counts employing that notion as a trademark of bad philosophizing (IHP 4). Making sense of Sartre's hostility to the notion of content will help substantially our understanding of his view of experience; it will also assist us in addressing crucial interpretative questions in the following chapters.[13]

Let us first distinguish between intentional and immanent content. "Intentional" is whatever pertains to the directedness of consciousness on its object. The intentional content of a conscious act is the object as intended by the particular act.[14] When we specify what an experience is about we refer to its intentional "matter". The intentional matter is what gives the act its grip on the object: it establishes a reference for the act, and identifies the act as being about this object, seen or imagined under this aspect, thought under this conception. Because in intending an object one is conscious of it as something, a reference to the matter of the act tells us how the object is meant; it gives us, in other words, the "meaning" of the act, or the sense in which something is intended in our experience (as a flower vase, or as a gift from my aunt, or as the only hand-painted object on my shelf, or as something made of fine china).[15] To be sure, an act is not exhausted by its matter, given that the same matter can be intended in many different ways such as perceiving, thinking, judging, doubting, wishing or imagining, all of which give us the "quality" of the particular act. Note, finally, that quality and matter are not self-subsistent entities; each feeds on the other, and can only be separated through abstraction from lived experience. Consider now that the same object can be intended at different moments, but in the same way, by the same subject. Those different intentions, being directed from the same standpoint toward the same object, share the same intentional content. The intentional matter of each of those acts is the same, yet the experiences are numerically different. To understand this basic phenomenon we need to refer to what is not shared by acts that have the same intentional content. We must, in other words, look at what is immanent to each occurrence of the various conscious acts. "Immanent" is whatever lies, as it were, on the side of consciousness: whatever can be counted as part, moment, phase, character, or feature of it. Any conscious act, such as thinking of a cube, is a real, subjective occurrence, that takes place in, or extends over, a period of time. Immanent content refers to the actual phases of conscious activity that make up a particular experience. Conscious acts intending the same object under the same aspect can have the same intentional matter but necessarily differ in their immanent content.

We may sum up the above distinctions by stating that whereas intentional content is what is intended by, presented to or meant by consciousness, immanent content is what is undergone by, or lived through, conscious experience. Drawing distinctions, however, is one thing; seeing how they can help us resolve philosophical issues is another. And a major issue here is the structure of intentional activity. It could be argued that intentionality denotes the relation of consciousness to what it is about; and what consciousness is about is its content.[16] Thus, the existence of content is a necessary condition of intentional activity, whereas the presence of an object is a welcome bonus.

This approach seems particularly well suited to phenomena of conscious activity directed towards what is not currently present. After all, it would be hard to deny that we may think of things that no longer exist (in memory), as well as of things that have not physically existed, or even could not physically exist (in imagination). One way to account for these phenomena is to keep separate the intentional object from the intentional content. We can thus dissociate the necessary relation between a thought and its content from the contingent connection between a thought and its intended object: intentionality requires that one is thinking something (that there is some content thought) whether or not that about which one is thinking actually exists.

Whatever the virtues of the above approach, it is not one Sartre would endorse at his first foray in the phenomenological maze. For Sartre, consciousness is a movement of fleeing oneself: to be conscious is to transcend oneself towards something. The very phenomenon of intentionality would be annulled if consciousness could not be directed upon anything. Given Sartre's interpretation of intentionality as transcendence, the idea of consciousness directing itself towards its content is absurd. But that is precisely what the notion of "content", as interpreted by Sartre at this stage, seems to require. For Sartre, the appeal to mental content plays straight into the hands of idealists. The suggestion that consciousness is directed towards mental content would sound plausible only if the mind were a non-material substance, including the pictures, ideas or replicas of material things:

> What is a table, a rock, a house? A certain assemblage of "contents of consciousness," a class of such contents. O digestive philosophy! Yet nothing seemed more obvious: is not the table the content of my perception? Is not my perception the present state of my consciousness? Nutrition, assimilation ... of things to ideas, of ideas by ideas, of minds by minds ... assimilation, unification, identification. (IHP 4)

The idealist fixation with mental immanence finds its contrary in Sartre's philosophy of transcendence (IHP 5). To be conscious of the world is not some intra-mental affair. As he plainly puts it, "to perceive is to bump against a presence".[17] The question remains, however, whether that philosophy can make sense of conscious phenomena where there seems to be nothing "out there" in the world towards which consciousness can be directed. Sartre's early approach is silent on this matter. In order to get a systematic answer, we shall need to explore Sartre's developed theory of imagination (see Chapter 5). In the remainder of this chapter, let us consider another important dimension of our experience of what is present.

V

The world as experienced is rarely neutral; things can be interesting or boring, provocative, frightening or simply charming. It is often claimed that none of these qualities characterizes things as they are; whatever significance a situation might have, it is something not encountered, but invented. However, that claim rings false to our experience. Sartre is unequivocal on this point: "it is things which abruptly unveil themselves to us as hateful, sympathetic, horrible, loveable" (IHP 5). This might appear problematic as an explanation of what it is for something to have positive or negative significance. However, Sartre is not presently advancing a theory about the nature of values. His concern is with the accurate description of reality as it is revealed in human experience. Under normal circumstances, the occurrence of an emotionally significant event precedes, and thus accounts for, our emotions *vis-à-vis* that event. We do not first feel fear and then notice something fearful, as we do not first feel surprised and then perceive something unexpected. Our sentiments are attuned to changes in reality, because they are a kind of perceptual state of those aspects of reality relevant to our concerns. The overall point of this analysis is that emotions are not the blind denizens of a spiritual realm, but "ways of discovering the world" (IHP 5).

The Sartrean approach sets itself against a subjectivist analysis of affective phenomena. The subjectivist, in this context, is someone who takes feeling to be some "purely subjective and ineffable shiver", enclosed within a subject whose affective experience is dissociated from the world of material and social interaction. Mechanical links between one's feeling and one's representation of the world are of course feasible, but they form at best only contingent associations that might lack any rhyme or reason (*IPPI* 67–8). Among the various kinds of subjectivism, Sartre singles out for consideration a theory that conceives of feeling as a direct apprehension of organic phenomena, whereby one becomes aware of changes in particular aspects, or in the overall state and posture of one's body. The details of this theory, and of the Sartrean objections to it, will occupy us in Chapter 4, when we consider Sartre's account of emotions. What is of direct relevance to the present discussion is that subjectivism severs consciousness from its object. Hence, the intentionality of feeling is ignored, and the emotional experience is isolated from its signification, producing the psychological counterpart of idealist metaphysics, that is "the solipsism of affectivity" (*IPPI* 68).

Feeling, no less than seeing, is a way in which consciousness aims at the world. Against the "*immanentist* prejudices of outdated psychology" (Sartre 1947: 63, emphasis added), Sartre affirms that feelings have special intentionalities; they are a way of transcending (*IPPI* 69). What is "special" about them is simply the fact that they cannot be reduced to, or substituted for, by other kinds of intentionality. Two errors are quite common on this point. The first is the intellectualist error of presenting feeling as a kind of propositional attitude – usually as a judgement on, or belief about, the affective object (IPPI 69). The second is to confuse the intentional structure of reflection on the feeling (how we think about the experience), with the intentionality involved in the feeling itself (how the world appears to us during the emotional episode.)[18]

Sartre's analysis of emotions is one of his lasting contributions in the history of philosophy. However, his early approach to emotions as in many ways similar to sense perceptions leaves open at least two questions. The first concerns the relation between emotions and feelings: what is the relation between, say, seeing that someone's behaviour is offensive, and actually feeling angry at the sight of him? Perception of a behaviour as offensive is not necessarily identical to being in a state of anger, and more needs to be said before we can interpret accurately the relation of emotion to perception. A second question concerns the relation between emotion and action. There is often a clear connection between the way one feels about someone and the way one behaves towards that person: it is not by pure coincidence that angry people might exchange blows instead of compliments. Yet it is not clear how emotions, as mere perceptions, can have the power to motivate our actions. The question of how emotion relates to behaviour is an intriguing one that would exercise Sartre for the best part of his philosophical career. At one point he argued for a thesis that sounds diametrically opposed to his initial view: "affectivity is [neither cognitive nor perceptual but] practical" (1960–85: 189). Giving both action and perception their dues is by no means an easy task in the phenomenology of emotion. As we shall see in Chapter 4, Sartre will try to address this problem by drawing attention to the embodied nature of consciousness as a key to the correct understanding of our perception of, and stance towards, the world.

VI

The sharp distinction between consciousness and the world is the source of Sartre's original take on intentionality, as well as the source of some of the problems we have mentioned. I think that these problems are indicative of an oscillation in Sartre's philosophical attitudes in the period leading up to his first article on intentionality.

On the one hand, he treats reality as an object of contemplative, almost aesthetic, curiosity, open to the fascinated gaze of a young philosopher who wishes nothing less than to survey the meaning of the totality of facts (*OR* 111; *CDG* 487). By his own lights, this approach was conducive to a "retreat *vis à vis* the objects of the world: I was contemplating them. I was nearby them. They were not extending to me, neither I to them" (quoted in Contat 1996: 461).

On the other hand, his sound refusal to treat consciousness as a substance, and the concomitant view that to be conscious is to fly out into the world, make Sartre a staunch critic of the idealist preoccupation with the empty cosiness of the human mind, as a privileged focus of philosophical understanding. The interpretation of intentionality as transcendence entails that everything on which consciousness is directed is outside consciousness: "everything, even ourselves. It is not in some hiding-place that we will discover ourselves; it is on the road, in the town, in the midst of the crowd, a thing among things, a man among men" (IHP 5). Whether this view is able to make sense of what it is to be oneself will be the topic of the next chapter.

CHAPTER THREE

The ego

I

Philosophical tradition has it that where there is thinking, there is an "I" that thinks. This "I" is sometimes seen as an entity dwelling within the mind, an immaterial substance whose activity constitutes our conscious life. Some other times, the "I" is considered as a formal principle that synthesizes disparate perceptions or ideas into complete thoughts. Either way, the I is at the heart of consciousness, sustaining the creation, reception and manipulation of mental content: without an I, conscious activity seems to collapse. Sartre thinks that tradition has it wrong: the I could not be residing inside consciousness since consciousness has no inside. If the I exists, it can only exist "outside, *in the world*" (*TE* 1; *LTE* 13).

The Latin transliteration of the first personal pronoun in Greek is "*ego*", and that is the favourite way for many philosophers to refer to important aspects of our self, both as the initiator of thoughts, volitions or actions – what I do – as well as the seat of sensations, feelings or passions – what occurs in me. Sartre's critique applies to both sides of the ego, with special emphasis on the ego as the alleged leader of our conscious life. For Sartre, the ego is not the subject of, but an object for consciousness and depends on the latter for its existence.

In reversing the traditional priorities between consciousness and the ego, Sartre employs some important distinctions between different modes of consciousness. Pre-reflective consciousness is the ordinary consciousness of objects in the world; reflective consciousness is the consciousness of being conscious of something. Pre-reflective consciousness is a *positional* consciousness of a certain object, in the sense that consciousness posits, sets before itself, the object as a target of its intentional activity. However, when one is positionally conscious of a particular object, one is *non-positionally* conscious of being conscious of that object. Pre-reflective consciousness is thus non-positionally aware of itself as being directed towards its objects. Let me explicate the meaning of the above terms, with the hope of averting some popular misunderstandings of the relevant distinctions.

II

In ordinary circumstances, when I pass by a garden looking at a rose, I am positionally conscious of the flower, without necessarily thinking to myself, "I am now looking at a flower". Indeed, while my sight is absorbed by the colour of the roses or the shape of the garden, I am not conscious of any "I" or "me" doing anything. I am, of course, aware of seeing the rose; if you ask me what I was doing I will truthfully answer that I was seeing a flower. And if, at a later point, I start thinking about the fact that I was seeing that object, then my attention is directed not at the rose, but on my act of seeing, that is now posited as the explicit object of my reflection. In reflection the act of seeing becomes the positional object of my thought, while at the pre-reflective level, the consciousness is non-positionally aware of its acts while being absorbed by the external focus of its attention.

According to the Sartrean account of consciousness, while I am perceiving an object I am conscious of perceiving it, without having to interrupt my activities so as to think explicitly about (and, in that sense, *posit* as a theme for my conscious activity) the fact that I perceive something. For Sartre every positional consciousness of an object is at the same time a non-positional consciousness of itself (cf. *BN* 9).

The distinction between positional and non-positional consciousness is a staple of phenomenological discourse about conscious awareness. The very commonness of that distinction, though, might make us lose sight of the fact that it employs terms that may be open to different interpretations. The standard way of analysing the relevant notions is by mapping the positional/non-positional distinction onto the focal/

peripheral distinction: just as one is peripherally aware of the things surrounding the object on which one is focused, so – the standard interpretation goes – in seeing something, the subject is peripherally aware of his seeing the object on which he is focused.[1] I believe that, despite its popularity, that interpretation of the positional/non-positional distinction is incorrect.

The focal/peripheral distinction is a distinction within one mode of awareness. In vision, the field of awareness may include several different items, all of which are perceptually organized around the spot (usually occupied by a single object) on which our sight is focused. What surrounds the object I am foveating lies in the periphery of my visual field. Peripheral awareness, in this example, is visual awareness of objects lying at the periphery of a space whose coordinates are determined through the relation between myself, as a perceiver, and the things perceived.

Note that what counts as focal and peripheral changes with the shifts in direction of the perceiver's visual intention: the pen, previously in the background among the other items lying to the right of the typewriter, is now the focal object of my perception. The basic explanation of that phenomenon is not hard to find. Perceiving is always the seizing of an object from out of a set of objects that are co-given. I do not see a typewriter, and then put a desk under it, a pen to its right, and a wall behind it. I take in visually a scene as a whole, and out of it a particular object stands as the figure against the background.

The details of how visual awareness works is a complex matter in the theory of perception. One point, however, is clear: that peripheral and focal vision are of the same kind of things, that is of perceptible, spatially located objects. And that is precisely what is not the case with the positional/non-positional pair. To stay with the phenomenon of vision, a positional consciousness is consciousness of the typewriter, whereas the non-positional consciousness is consciousness of my looking at that object. Non-positionally, I am not aware of one or another perceptible object but of my perceiving of objects. We may express the distinction by saying that positionally we are aware of objects, and that non-positionally we are aware of our experience of those objects.

The assimilation of the positional/non-positional distinction to the focal/peripheral distinction is, I believe, indicative of what Sartre described as "our habit of thinking in space and in terms of space" (*IPPI* 5). A better way of understanding the relation between those two distinctions is by noting that both the focal vision and peripheral vision operate within the positional awareness of the world. To return to our example, my looking at the typewriter includes the perceptual awareness of a number of other objects that surround the typewriter, and are thus lying at the periphery of my visual field. My consciousness intends an object, the typewriter, in its perceptual context. I am positionally aware of a perceptible scene that includes several items, one of which is in focus, with the rest at the periphery of the visual field. Yet, throughout that experience, I am (non-positionally) conscious of my being (positionally) conscious of the typewriter (focally), and of the desk, pen, wall and so on (peripherally). Failure to appreciate these points gives a mistaken view not only of the self-representationalist's positional/non-positional distinction, but also of the basic structure of visual experience.

It is worth noting that an analogous problem arises if we define non-positional consciousness as supposedly encompassing anything that falls within our field of awareness but to which we are not currently paying attention.[2] The suggested identification of non-attentiveness with non-positionality is, I believe, equally incorrect. Usually, the object that lies at the centre of my foveal vision is also the object of my attention (usually, although not always: I may be foveating the typewriter in front of me, yet paying attention to the news bulletin that just interrupted the music stream on the radio). Assuming, as is often the case, that what I am focusing on is what I am attending to, I remain positionally aware of several items in my environment (the desk, the walls, the smell of ink, or the radio commercials), to which I am not paying any attention.[3]

We perceive something attentively when we engage with it in a certain way. Among the things I currently perceive, some are sufficiently salient to me to attract my attention. Talk of attention signifies that the subject is actively involved in the collecting and processing of information concerning items or events of which she is positionally aware. Hence, the distinction between "attentively" and "non-attentively being conscious of something" can be drawn within the domain of objects of which one is positionally conscious. Therefore, that something is not the object of my attention does not *ipso facto* imply that I am non-positionally aware of it; it can just be part of the scene of which I am positionally conscious, without it being the focus of my attention. However, there is a truth in the claim that non-positional awareness is non-attentive, in the precise sense that ordinarily in being positionally aware of, for example, what I am typing, I am not attending to my experience of my typing it (of my touching the keys, scanning the screen for errors, thinking through the next sentence, etc.). What occupies my attention is what I type, or, at most, the typewriter, and not my seeing it.

Let me sum up the discussion of this section by briefly stating its main results. The Sartrean theory of consciousness asserts that in being positionally conscious of an object, for example in perception, I am non-positionally conscious of my perceiving it. The standard way of explicating that assertion is by means of equating the "non-positional" either with the "non-focal" or with the "non-attentive".[4] I believe that neither equation is appropriate. The focal/peripheral distinction is applicable within the domain of the positional awareness of, for example, perceptible items in our environment through vision. The attentive/non-attentive distinction also signifies how the subject engages with certain of the items of which she is positionally aware. Therefore, non-positional consciousness is identical to neither non-focal nor non-attentive consciousness. Making proper sense of that distinction will not be helped by reducing it to something it is not.[5]

III

Sartre employs the positional/non-positional, attentive/non-attentive and reflective/non-reflective distinctions to maximum effect in arguing against the alleged necessity of an ego for the life of consciousness. His argumentation has divided scholars for decades, as some commentators see in him the forerunner of the deconstruction of the self, while others confirm him as the last great defender of the primacy of the human subject. In the specific text that we shall explore here, the truth is perhaps less exciting, but conceptually more subtle. On the one hand, Sartre asserts that the I appears in reflection, it presents itself to us, it is given to our intuition (*TE* 43, 53); hence, it could not be easily dismissed as an accident of our grammar, or a figment of our cultural imagination (see e.g. Bard 2002: 9). On the other hand, he effectively undermines the view that the ego is always present in our mental life, lurking behind every conscious move: the I comes "after the fact", when consciousness turns its attention to its acts and thinks of a particular being as the locus of certain thoughts, perceptions, feelings or actions.

His detailed critique of the ego lies mainly in the claim that conscious activity does not need the ego; indeed, placing an ego within consciousness deprives the latter of its lucidity, and renders the intentional opening to the world problematic. The overall point of his discussion is that if consciousness is to be a genuine transcendence towards the world, then the ego of philosophical tradition ought to be transcended.

Undermining the well-entrenched belief in the reality of the ego is not an easy task. Sartre will try two main lines of attack. On the one hand, he argues that the ego is not required for explaining the unity and individuality of consciousness. On the other hand, he shows that, as traditionally understood, installing an ego in our mental life would mark the death of consciousness. Let us examine each point in turn.

IV

However different they might be, the various perceptions, thoughts or feelings that make up my conscious life have one thing in common: they are all mine. An explanation of this basic fact should account for the unity of consciousness: what makes different conscious acts part of one consciousness?

The question of unity involves several issues that should be carefully distinguished: (i) the unity that characterizes each conscious act at any one time; (ii) the unity of different conscious acts intending the same object at different times; (iii) the unity of a conscious process unfolding in time; and (iv) the unity of all conscious acts that make up my stream of consciousness through time.

What gives unity to a conscious act at any one time is the object intended in the act. At each moment I intend an object, the conscious act unifies itself by transcending itself towards the particular object. In looking at a cube, my seeing is unified by intending a unified object, the particular individual entity. The cube, as a material entity, is unified independently of my seeing it, and the unity of the particular conscious act is due to, rather than a cause for, the unity of that object. The same, according to Sartre, applies in the case of abstract objects: the unity of my thought that two and two make four is due to the unity of the mathematical truth "two and two make four". That two and two make four is an eternal truth, characterized by a permanence that sets this transcendent object opposite my consciousness (*TE* 38). My intention encounters the mathematical object, whose existence manifests itself in my thought, bestowing on it any meaning and unity it has. After all, the thought that two and two make four is just a consciousness transcending itself towards a mathematical truth, which identifies that *thought* for what it is, namely, the thought that two and two make four.

The account of unity of a conscious act at any one time is carried over to the case of the unity of different conscious acts intending the same object at different times: the unity of all the conscious acts by which I have added, add, and will add two and two to make four "is the transcendent object 'two and two make four'" (*TE* 38).

Sartre's example is quite straightforward. Consciousness finds its unity in the intentional object. This approach implies that the unity of the intentional object does not depend on the consciousness that intends it. And it is this last implication that could make one reluctant to take Sartre at his own word. It has thus been proposed that what Sartre should mean is not that our consciousness aims at a (unified) object, but that, instead, it is consciousness that creates, say, the mathematical truth that two and two make four, and bestows on the mathematical proposition its unity. As this reading is in direct contrast to the spirit of Sartre's own example, the reinterpretation continues with the claim that, perhaps, what Sartre really has in mind is a two-way dependence: the unity of the intentional object depends on the unity of a conscious act, which becomes unified by aiming at a unified object, which was not unified before consciousness aimed at it. The circularity generated by this reading is rather hard to avoid.[6] It is worth asking, therefore, what could motivate such an interpretation.

One answer might be the temptation to fill any gaps in Sartre's argumentation by invoking a different theory of the relation between consciousness and its intentional objects, whether or not that theory is in tune with the rest of Sartre's own approach to the issue at hand. This temptation becomes irresistible if we also think that, by leaving the young Sartre to his own devices, we end up with an account of the unity of consciousness that commits us to the reality of not only physical, but also abstract, mathematical objects. However, in matters of accurate interpretation, neither of these considerations provides sufficient grounds for revising Sartre's own approach to the dependence of consciousness on its objects. What accounts for the unity of conscious acts is the intentional opening of consciousness to objects that, contrary to the subjectivist preconceptions of many philosophers, consciousness could never have created out of the empty cosiness of the human mind. The object is not unified by consciousness; rather, "it is in the object that the unity of consciousness is found" (*TE* 38).

V

Another aspect of the issue of unity concerns the unity of a conscious activity through time. This unity is necessary if we are to be able to encounter transcendent objects that exist outside our stream of consciousness. A transcendent object, such as a large wooden box, is a temporal object in the sense that it persists for some time. If I move around to look at each one of its visible sides, I am aware of encountering different aspects of the same object. That would be impossible if each momentary experience I had of a surface dropped out of my consciousness while another experience of another surface took over completely; in that case I would not be having the experience of different aspects of the same physical object, but rather a succession of instantaneous experiences of unconnected surfaces.

The unity of conscious activity permeates all sense modalities, and it is clearly evident in the experience of hearing a melody. As the record is playing, if all I were conscious of were an instantaneous tone, and at another instance a tone, and at another instance a tone and so on, I would not be having the experience of a melody, but of sound coming in and out of existence. (Even this would concede too much: to have a sense of a particular sound just starting you should be aware of the nonexistence of the sound before that instant, yet that would be impossible if I were not able in the present to have a sense of the immediate past.) The experience of a melody involves a synthesis of sound sensations through time; the musical piece is built up of tones succeeding other tones paving the way for other tones, in the unceasing, seamless unity of my consciousness of sound in my environment. That I now hear a piece of music is due to the fact that my primal impression of a tone is affected by tones just passed, yet retained in my consciousness in a way that makes me experience the melody.

While transcendent objects exist in time, conscious experience unfolds in time. The temporal thread that runs through experience is precisely what makes possible the connection of the current consciousness with the just past, yet presently retained, consciousness of the intentional object. A particular conscious activity is itself an integral part of the stream of our consciousness. The unity of our consciousness as a whole is found in the temporal interplay of our sensations, thoughts, emotions or desires: "consciousness refers constantly back to itself, whoever says 'a consciousness' means the whole of consciousness" (*TE* 39). Our consciousness unifies itself through time, thanks to the web of relations that exist between our experiences, past and present (*LTE* 22).

Sartre's discussion of the question of unity is brief and to the point: we can account for the unity of consciousness without making the slightest reference to an ego. The "I" plays no role in bringing our conscious activities together. Faithful to his critique of idealism, and of the traditional preoccupation with the powers of an ego that supposedly lies within or behind our consciousness, Sartre maintains that consciousness takes care of itself through temporal relations that link conscious acts intending the world. As he succinctly puts it: "consciousness unifies itself by escaping from itself" (*TE* 38).

VI

If the ego is redundant in the explanation of the unity of consciousness, can it fare any better with the explanation of the individuality of consciousness, the fact that each consciousness is different from another? Sartre's answer is in the negative: no appeal to an ego is necessary, since the fact of individuality is explained by the nature of consciousness itself.

A consciousness involves intentional openings towards the world, and transversal relations that run through the intentional acts as conscious activity unfolds in time. The particular ways in which the world is revealed to each consciousness, and the particularity of the innumerable combinations through which these intentions are synthesized in the flow of experience, account for the fact that each consciousness, being a "synthetic totality" of its conscious acts, is different: they account, in other words for its individuality.

At the ordinary, non-reflective level of experience, each consciousness is non-positionally aware of itself being conscious of various objects. This awareness is non-positional in the sense that the object posited as the focus of one's experience is not one's own consciousness but something outside consciousness towards which consciousness is directed. The non-positional awareness of itself is not a form of knowledge that consciousness has about itself. To be conscious of itself, consciousness does not need to check for relevant evidence that would give it sufficient epistemic grounds for forming the belief that it is aware of being conscious of its intentional objects: consciousness does not infer its awareness of itself.

The unreflected consciousness's (non-positional) awareness of itself is available only to that consciousness. It is this fact that gives consciousness a hold on the notion of ownership of its conscious activities, its sense of inwardness (*TE* 40).

The above analysis offers a plausible case for Sartre's approach on this matter. His explicit discussion of the individuality of consciousness is given in a short paragraph that has given rise to several interpretations, each one exploiting different remarks on the question of individuality found in different parts of Sartre's text, or even in different Sartrean texts. The laconic character of his analysis is perhaps the major obstacle in reaching a unanimous agreement on how exactly we should reconstruct Sartre's reasoning. However, one point appears to be well established by a careful reading of the text: it concerns the role of the body in the individuation of consciousness. It has been suggested that each consciousness is different from another because it is limited by its bodily bearer, each consciousness being connected to a different body. So generally put this claim is not incorrect, but it does not illuminate Sartre's distinctive approach on this issue. In *The Transcendence of the Ego* the body is strikingly absent. It does not make any appearance in the discussion of why each consciousness is different from the other. When the body is addressed by Sartre it is only in order to have it dismissed as part of an explanation of why we cannot apprehend each others' consciousness the way we do our own. The reason, for Sartre, is not that the body allegedly hides the other's psychological states from view, but the very interiority of one's non-positional consciousness of itself: "the fact that each consciousness is aware of itself from the inside" (*TE* 66–7).

However, we may need to accept that the body enters the Sartrean argumentation through a different route. Recall that the individuality of consciousness is implied by the particular way in which each consciousness has been an intentional opening to the world, and the particular relations running through the whole of consciousness synthesizing all of its unique yet innumerable acts into a unified stream of consciousness. But how is this particularity to be understood if not as a consequence of the finite perspective that each consciousness enjoys owing to its spatiotemporal standpoint? I would suggest that the role of the body in the unity and individuality of consciousness plays a discreet yet significant role, which will be drawn out explicitly at a later stage in Sartre's philosophical career (see *BN* III, ch. 2).[7]

VII

The Sartrean analysis sidesteps the standard move of the traditional account of individuality of consciousness, according to which one consciousness differs from another because each one supposedly belongs to a different ego. Except for its circularity as an alleged ground for the reality of the ego, such an account would make consciousness dependent on something that, according to Sartre, is antithetical to the possibility of conscious activity.

The ego is supposedly a substance that exists within consciousness. The ego is thus for consciousness an object towards which consciousness, as the very appearing of any object, is directed. While consciousness is all "clear and lucid", an object is necessarily "opaque", since it is that concrete or abstract target of intentional activity, gradually revealed to us through its various aspects. Consciousness is (nothing but consciousness of itself as) a revelation of the intentional object. Placing an ego within consciousness would thus cancel the essential features of conscious activity. Consciousness would not be the spontaneous directedness towards objects in thought, perception or imagination, but it would be run by a control centre inaccessible to consciousness. Most importantly, consciousness would cease to be the immediate, pre-reflective, non-thetic awareness of itself; it would instead have to negotiate its way around a substance that could not only hide itself from consciousness, but could also make consciousness hide from its own view.

The introduction of a mental or material substance within consciousness would make darkness fall in the field of lucidity. If it existed, the ego "would tear consciousness from itself" precisely because "it would slide into every consciousness like an opaque blade" (*TE* 40).

For Sartre, the alleged presence of a substantial ego runs counter to the reality of consciousness as a non-substantial absolute. Consciousness is absolute in the phenomenological sense that its consciousness of itself is not dependent on anything other than itself. To be sure, consciousness is metaphysically dependent on its intentional objects, since in the absence of objects to be revealed consciousness would cease to be an intentional opening to the world. However, while it is thus dependent on the existence of intentional objects, it is not dependent on anything else for being conscious of itself being conscious of objects.

Why, though, is consciousness a non-substantial absolute? As we have already seen, consciousness belongs to a different category than substance: as a directedness towards objects, it is not a thing, but the revealing of things. We may now see a further reason for Sartre's refusal to think of the field of conscious activity as the domain of a mental or material substance. In the case of consciousness, being and appearing coincide in a way that is not possible for substances. Sartrean realism requires that substances may in principle transcend our knowledge or awareness of them. A substance is not dependent on how, if at all, it may appear to us. Consciousness, on the other hand, cannot be consciousness without appearing to itself non-positionally even in its unreflected moments.

It could be argued that Sartre's critique of the ego is misguided, since the ego might not be a material or spiritual substance, but a mere structure of consciousness. We may respond that, as a matter of historical accuracy, the philosophers criticized by Sartre do appear to commit themselves to the alleged reality of a substantial ego. His opponents are not theoretical straw men but the authors of important works with which Sartre's own text is engaged in critical dialogue.[8] Furthermore, the idea of an ego as a structure of consciousness is rather ambiguous. On the one hand, it could simply refer to the way conscious activity happens to process information or to unfold in time, in which case Sartre might accept such a revised notion of an ego as a structure carrying no explanatory or metaphysical weight. On the other hand, if we think of structure as something imposed on consciousness from outside itself, over which consciousness has no access on how or why it guides conscious activity, and which could control consciousness's non-thetic awareness of itself, then the same criticism directed against the idea of a substantial ego would apply to the idea of the ego as structure.

All in all, Sartre has argued that the ego is redundant in the explanation of the unity and individuality of consciousness, and is antithetical to the spontaneity and lucidity that essentially characterizes conscious activity. Is it still possible to rescue the traditional analysis of the ego as the real subject of experience? It seems that the supporter of the ego might respond by what appears initially to be the major obstacle to the Sartrean view of consciousness: the fact that the I does appear to consciousness each time consciousness effects the *cogito*.

VIII

"*Cogito*" is the first person indicative of "*cogitare*", the Latin word for thinking. It implies the first-person personal pronoun "*ego*" and along with it a host of philosophical manoeuvres aimed to establish the reality of the latter, by drawing on the phenomenological certainty of the thinking consciousness. Sartre is happy to acknowledge that when one's consciousness is focusing on one's mental activities, the *cogito* appears to be personal: "In the I Think there is an I who thinks" (*TE* 43). Where he parts company with the tradition, though, is in his analysis of how the *cogito* is itself possible.

In thinking or stating that "I think" ("I see", "I touch", "I remember", "I imagine"), my consciousness is focusing on my experience and reports, registers or in general reflects on its conscious activity. Thus the activities of thinking, perceiving, imagining and so on become the explicit focus of my awareness, making conscious activity itself the positional object of my consciousness. The *cogito* is effected by the reflecting consciousness on the (up to that moment unreflected, but currently) reflected consciousness.

The expression "I think" ("I see", "I remember", etc.) points to an occurrence in the stream of consciousness reflected on by the reflecting consciousness. The "I think" ("I see", "I remember", etc.) belongs to the reflected consciousness that is currently the object of my conscious attention. Drawing a clear distinction between the reflecting consciousness and the reflected consciousness will help us realize that "the consciousness which says I Think is precisely not the consciousness which thinks", but the consciousness that reports that occurrence at the level of the reflected consciousness (*TE* 45). However, and that is the crucial point, the reflecting consciousness is not accompanied by an I: only the reflected consciousness carries an I on its sleeve while, and in so far as, it is not a live part of conscious activity but a positional object for it.

Sartre offers a brief example to illustrate his point: "If ... I want to remember a certain landscape perceived yesterday from the train, it is possible to bring back the memory of that landscape as such. But I can also recollect that I was seeing that landscape" (*TE* 42). We may employ our analysis of the Sartrean approach in order to interpret that example as follows.

Yesterday, while I was travelling on the train, looking out of the window, my consciousness was absorbed by the landscape. It was a positional consciousness of the mountain and the fields, and a non-positional awareness of itself as perceptual consciousness of the landscape. At all those moments it was an unreflected, intentional opening to the world, and no ego appeared anywhere, neither in nor behind, consciousness.

Now that I recall the event, my memory can furnish a number of different objects. I can simply remember the mountains and green fields: in that case, my consciousness is still positionally directed to the world, it is unreflected, and no I appears on the horizon. Second, I can focus on my looking at the fields. The object of my memory becomes the activity of looking at something: the positional object of my current consciousness is my past perceptual consciousness of the landscape. It is not that the landscape has suddenly disappeared from view – such a disappearance of an intentional object would mean the end of the perceptual consciousness – but that my consciousness is now engaged with its perceiving something at an earlier moment in time. My perceptual awareness of the landscape is the reflected consciousness on which my current consciousness is reflecting. Third, my consciousness can be directed on the fact that it was I who was looking out of the train window at the landscape.

In that case, my consciousness, reflecting on its past occurrences, focuses on the I as its intentional object. The I is phenomenologically evident as the positional object of the reflecting consciousness.

The *cogito* belongs to the reflected consciousness; both the "I" and the "think" of the "I think" belong to past consciousness as it is reflected on by current consciousness. However, the "I" is not the same kind of thing as "thinking". The latter is a kind of activity lasting a certain period of time, and that leaves an unreflected, non-positional memory, on which my present consciousness is reflecting. The former is an abstract entity arising in the very act of reflecting on the activity. Sartre adduces a phenomenological reason for drawing this distinction. Whereas the various occurrences of my thinking (seeing, touching, imagining, etc.) appear as perishable moments of conscious experience, the I appears to have a permanence exceeding any one of those moments. Indeed, the ego is never given at once to my reflection: it is an elusive and opaque object that I cannot pretend to grasp as a whole just by mentioning one of my past activities. It gradually unfolds its presence while I reflect on past experience, in the same way as any other object that appears to consciousness through different aspects.

A privileged view into the nature of that supposedly mysterious entity is offered through consideration of our past actions, character qualities and emotional experiences. In the central sections of the next chapter we shall see in detail how Sartre analyses the emotional aspects of our psychological life. The main point, though, of his approach can be briefly stated here as follows. When we think and talk about our experience, the life of consciousness is considered under certain headings, such as "qualities of character", "mental or physical acts" and "emotional states". Those headings impose some order on past conscious experience, transforming continuous instances of perpetual activity into isolable states. Those past states are, in their turn, being thought to emanate from the ever-flowing spring of the ego. In that way, the ego is presented as the source of states, instantiated in particular activities. However, this picture presents conscious experience the wrong way round. What comes first is the conscious activity directed at the world. The psychological state follows, as the outcome of grouping activities under one heading; that grouping generates psychological categories that transcend consciousness, in the sense that those states appear as fixed entities with set boundaries, which share nothing of the fluid and luminous character of conscious activity. Those transcendent psychological states are then conceived as members of one psychological whole that embraces every aspect of our mental life. In an apt metaphor, Sartre writes that the ego stands to psychological states in the way the world stands to its objects: a world transcends individual objects, and yet, in their total absence, there would be nothing for a world to be a world of. Like the external world of transcended objects intended by perceptual consciousness, the ego intended by reflection is the transcendent pole of unity of psychological states. Before we examine how this process operates in the case of emotional states, let us take stock of the main claims made in this chapter.

The first major point of Sartre's phenomenological enquiry is that the ordinary unreflected consciousness is impersonal, in the sense that it includes no "ego":

> When I run after a streetcar, when I look at the time, when I am absorbed in contemplating a portrait, there is no I. There is consciousness of the street car having to be overtaken, etc. and non-positional consciousness of consciousness. In fact, I am then plunged in the world of objects. (*TE* 49)

Second, although impersonal, each consciousness is individual. It has an immanent unity through time thanks to the particular way it is directed towards the world, and the transversal links that run through past and present activities that make up the stream of one's consciousness.

Next to that immanent unity, there is a transcendent unity of conscious acts that appears through the act of reflection. That transcendent unity is aptly expressed in claiming that "I think", "I see", "I remember" and so on. However, the I is not an accident of grammar. Nowhere in the present context does Sartre maintain that language simply plays a trick on us by imposing on consciousness something that would otherwise fail to exist. On the contrary, he asserts that the I is given to our intuition while consciousness focuses on its activities: "I can always perform a recollection whatsoever in the personal mode, and at once the I appears" (*TE* 43–4).

Finally, that unity is transcendent because it is an object for, rather than an integral part of, conscious activity. As a transcendent object, it is not transparent to consciousness but opaque, appearing in different profiles, always revealing itself through various aspects, but never contained as a whole in any one of the past thoughts, actions, feelings or perceptions that make up one's conscious life. The transcendent unity of all conscious acts reflected on by current consciousness is precisely that abstract object that traditional philosophy erroneously takes as the subject of conscious activity: "the ego, of which the I and the me are but two aspects, constitutes the ideal and indirect ... unity of the infinite series of our reflected consciousnesses" (*TE* 60).

But how exactly are our thoughts, feelings and actions involved in the constitution of our "psychological life"? The answer to this question will lead us to the discussion of one of the most celebrated parts of Sartre's early philosophy: his sketch for a theory of the emotions.

CHAPTER FOUR

Emotion

I

Sketch for a Theory of the Emotions (hereafter, the *Sketch*) has acquired classic status as an original analysis of emotional phenomena, yet its exact position in the philosophical debate over the nature of emotions is hard to determine. It is often argued that Sartre conceives of emotions as actions, but, given the implausibility of such a conception, his sketch can be rescued only by showing that what it outlines is not a general theory of emotion, but an analysis of emotional behaviour (see Barnes 1997; Neu 2000; Solomon 2003).

We shall see in this chapter that the standard line of interpretation is incorrect. Sartre draws a theoretical outline, whose subject matter is emotion in general, rather than only a particular aspect of it. His theory is immune to the main criticisms directed against it, since – selective readings to the contrary – it denies that emotions are actions. Most importantly, the value of his approach lies not so much in the defence of a particular camp in the current debates, as in the attempt to redefine what it is we do when we offer a philosophical account of emotions.

The analysis of these issues requires a clear grasp of the Sartrean conception of psychological states. I shall, accordingly, begin with a brief account of the Sartrean view of those states, followed by a presentation of the Sartrean critique of some classic theories of emotion, which will then take us to the analysis of the reasoning behind the claim that emotions are ways of apprehending the world (*STE* 35–6). Our discussion will be informed by the Sartrean idea that the philosophical analysis of emotions should enquire about what an emotion signifies: what it indicates for the life of the person who experiences the emotion, and which aspect of reality is indicated when the person is emotionally directed towards the world.

II

At the time of Sartre's writing on those topics, the question of significance had been largely neglected in the psychological literature on emotions.[1] That neglect was not due to an oversight on the part of otherwise highly systematic researchers of psychic phenomena. It stemmed rather from the very method employed in approaching those phenomena. That method starts with a collection of facts on the basis of observed similarities; it isolates each of those facts for examination, groups facts under various headings, and then reassembles large psychic sections by drawing connections between affect and other psychic parts such as cognition, belief, desire, intention and certain pieces of behaviour. The way in which these psychic bits link together is, to this date, the main point of dispute in the literature, with some theoreticians arguing for a chain of command that starts with cognition and, passing through affect, concludes in behaviour, while others are favouring a physiological train of events setting off at neural receptors and leading all the way up to indefinable, yet powerful feelings.[2]

Although Sartre is happy to engage with the finer points of that debate, he is primarily interested in questioning – with a view to illuminate – the theoretical assumptions under which the debating parties operate. A major assumption is that emotions are discrete, self-enclosed states: they constitute isolable units that can be added to or subtracted from the sum of psychic entities. As psychic states, emotions appear accidental to a researcher interested in the fact that they occur, but not in why they do so. The occurrence of an emotion is a fact, and facts do not hold a key to secret meanings. Indeed, by themselves they do not mean anything at all, or, rather, they mean nothing independently of what a researcher, driven by the desire for systematization, resolves to attribute to them.

It could be retorted that the Sartrean diagnosis is based on an overnarrow conception of psychological research into the emotions. Some of the best work in this area has recently brought the question of significance to the forefront of systematic enquiry, with specific proposals on the instrumental value of emotions in affecting the stance of others towards oneself (Griffiths 2003). My response to this objection is twofold. On the one hand, the Sartrean approach welcomes the emphasis on the strategic role of emotions; in fact, Sartre's approach can be considered as a philosophical predecessor of current research programmes on the negotiating power of emotions in social interaction.[3] On the other hand, the Sartrean approach is going beyond those research programmes by enabling us to reflect on the conception of emotions underpinning psychological research. The issue, in other words, is not how well Sartre reconstructs the psychological research of his date; as a matter of fact, he was one of the few philosophers to study, and participate in projects of experimental psychology. The point is whether a research programme based on certain theoretical assumptions can advance our understanding of emotions. And the Sartrean answer is that it cannot, because *an emotion is not a clog of mental machinery, but how the whole of consciousness operates in a certain situation*. In order to evaluate Sartre's views on this issue, let us look more closely at his conception of psychic states.

III

Our psychic states, such as boredom, jealousy or hatred, appear as psychic objects when we reflect on our past mental or physical activities, our actions, judgements or feelings. Take, for instance, the relation between the feeling of revulsion and the state of hatred. Feeling revulsion at the sight of a particular person is an experience absorbed with the detestable qualities of that individual. Experienced as a direct engagement with the world, the upheaval of a particular feeling towards someone marks the intentional connection between my consciousness and that being. The feeling of revulsion is a conscious activity occurring instantaneously or through a limited time span, and one that meets Sartre's absolute principle of consciousness, that is, to be an instant of felt revulsion and to feel as an instant of revulsion are one and the same thing: there is no gap within the "consciousness (of) revulsion" between appearing and being.

The genitive construction "consciousness (of) revulsion" might give the impression that in the course of ordinary encounter with the world there is a thing called "revulsion", to which consciousness pays attention. That interpretation is misleading. Revulsion is not an object for consciousness; it is consciousness itself as it experiences its intentional object. The genitive participle "of" is put in brackets so as to signal that the grammatical construction purports to characterize what a particular consciousness is (namely, revulsion), not what the consciousness is about (its intentional object, the particular person who just started addressing a political rally). Similarly, the locution "consciousness (of) despair" denotes, in the present context, a "despairing consciousness" – how an agent experiences a world where all possibilities are barred – not that his experience is about a certain object called "despair".

However, if we were to move from the plane of emotional encounter with the world, to the higher level of reflection on that type of encounter, our consciousness could take in its purview the emotion-consciousness. At that level, revulsion or other emotional experiences would themselves become an object of conscious examination and, thus, the locution "consciousness of revulsion" (free of internal brackets) would denote the second-order activity of consciousness focusing on its conscious activities. The confusion of the first-order level of the (revulsive, despairing or joyous) experience of the world with the second-order level of the consideration of such an experience by the (reflective) subject is a major source of difficulty for the adequate analysis of emotional phenomena.

The confusion of levels is itself the outcome of two kinds of pressure. The first stems from the unobjectionable claim that people are aware of having various emotions. That claim is taken to entail that what people are conscious of during an emotional episode is their own feelings. However, the latter claim is much stronger than, and it does not on its own follow upon, the former claim. To effect the transition one should draw on the dubitable principle that one cannot be aware of *x*, unless *x* is the explicit object of conscious attention. Sartre repudiates this view on two grounds. On the one hand, it falls foul of the phenomenology of conscious experience. On the other hand, it entangles consciousness in an infinite recurrence of reflective acts, on pain of rendering conscious experience unconscious.

According to Sartre, consciousness is at each moment (non-positionally) aware of itself being (positionally) aware of its intentional object. Looking at a squirrel involves the direct (positional) awareness of the furry animal, and the indirect (non-positional, although no less real) awareness of looking at it. Likewise, a "consciousness (of) revulsion" at the sight of a particular person involves the (positional) perception of him, and the simultaneous, indirect (non-positional, although no less significant) awareness of itself intending that person in a particular way.

Note, finally, that consciousness's (non-positional) awareness of itself need not be cast in conceptual terms. Hence, it is not a consequence of the Sartrean approach that to be aware of feeling a particular way towards someone, one should conceive of his feeling under a particular heading. All that the present view implies is that for an experience to be conscious it need not take itself as its intentional object. For Sartre, a particular experience of revulsion is simply a conscious experience that is appropriately focused on a detestable person, that is, on something other than the experience itself.

The above considerations remove part of the pressure for treating consciousness's encounter with the world as an instance of consciousness's reflective preoccupation with itself. However, the alleged importance of reflective activity is apparent not only in the context of theoretical debates, but also in the way we ordinarily think and talk about emotional phenomena. To understand how this works, we need to look closer at the Sartrean interpretation of emotional states.

IV

In ordinary discourse about psychological phenomena, emotional states are marked by a fixity and duration that transcends the fleeting nature of emotional feelings. The state of hatred may extend well beyond the instantaneous encounter with the repulsive person, as it underpins past feelings of disgust, aversion or anger towards him over a period of days, weeks or even years. It is thus thought to continue to exist even when I am absorbed in different activities, and to make its appearance each time it finds an expression at the prompting of events that present me with the detestable person. Hatred is not exhausted by a particular episode of feeling revulsion: the state was here yesterday when the feeling was not, and it might be here tomorrow well after my feeling has ceased to exist. To move from the claim "I am feeling revulsion while looking at him" to the claim "I hate him" is to perform a passage to infinity: to state that you hate someone is, in essence, to give your verdict on what your feelings towards him meant in the past and to express a commitment as to how you are to think, feel or act towards that person in the future.

In all these respects, the psychic state is more akin to perceivable objects than to the immanent activities of consciousness. In the same way that a physical object appears through different aspects, none of which exhausts the object in its entirety, the psychic state appears in and by each upheaval of feelings or actions, as it is thought to endure, in contrast to the feelings' transient occurrence.

Psychic states lie midway between consciousness and the realm of physical objects. According to Sartre, a psychic state appears when a reflective consciousness turns its attention on past conscious activities and surveys those consciousnesses under the heading of a particular concept. The state is a relative being, depending for its existence on the reflective gaze on the ordinary conscious experience of things or events in the world. However, in a reversal of actual priorities, the reflectively created state is taken to underlie one's feelings, thoughts and actions. The state appears as the principle that ties together various activities of consciousness, and holds the meaning of one's relation to the world. The analysis of that relation thus becomes an exploration of the allegedly hidden meaning of conscious experience. Our feelings, thoughts and actions provide clues to the mechanics of each psychic state that acts on the agent as a physical force, accounting for her past attitude and conditioning her future stance. Hence, the aim of the scientist of psychic states is to try to uncover the meaning of the state through the psychoanalysis of verbal and physical behaviour, viewed as the external coat of inner psychic entities. On this point, some trends in cognitive psychology and in classical psychoanalysis concur in their view of emotional states as entities to which the agent can have only restricted access, and over which she may enjoy very limited control.

The vocabulary of passivity that permeates much of the folk and scientific discourse on emotions reflects a conception of human beings as governed by entities dwelling somewhere between the spontaneous activities of the stream of consciousness, on the one hand, and the bodily constitution of our interaction with the world, on the other. That space in between the mental and the physical is that of the psychological, whose dual character speaks to the paradoxical nature of emotional states: passive yet purposive, involuntary but intentional, evaluative no less than physiological.

The occurrence of paradox might be a warning against setting psychic states as the starting-point of a philosophical enquiry into emotional phenomena. However, that is not the main objection that Sartre reserves for the standard view of emotions. The real problem, for Sartre, is that zooming in on psychic states produces theoretical short-sightedness. Psychic states cannot be studied independently of human nature and the world in general, since the psychic facts that we meet in our research are never prior: "they, in their essential structure, are reactions of man to the world: they therefore presuppose man and the world, and cannot take on their true meaning unless those two notions have first been elucidated" (*STE* 7–8).

That elucidation should interrogate the events under consideration with a view to comprehending their meaning. The interpretation of the meaning will enable us to understand the nature and identity of emotions, since what an emotion is depends on how it is lived by consciousness. The emotion of joy would not be what it is if it did not appear as joy to consciousness. The counterfactual here does not depict an epistemic relation between the first-order experience of emotion and a second-order reflective consciousness on it; it refers, rather, to the structure of the non-reflective first-order experience that is the emotional consciousness, including the non-positional awareness of itself – my joy at my friend's return is about him not about my consciousness.

Sartre conceives of his sketch for a theory of the emotions as an experiment in phenomenological psychology. Its subject matter is the human being in situation, and its objective is to identify the essence of emotional phenomena by showing how embodied consciousness constitutes their meaning.

V

The meaning of an emotion is the main casualty in the first classic theory Sartre examines. The "peripheric" theory is thus called because it locates the source of the emotion in the periphery of mental activity, namely in the body. Information about our bodies can take many forms: we can hear our voices in family recordings, see X-rays of our bones, or read the levels of our blood sugar in a diagram. However, some of the changes in our bodies are directly registered by consciousness: the tension in our muscles, the trembling of our hands, or the racing of our heart is lived by consciousness, while it is taking place. For the peripheric theory, the feeling of such somatic changes as they occur is the emotion.

Feelings are at the core of emotional experience, and perhaps no theory of emotions can do away with them.[4] One would be right to claim that what an emotion is depends on what it is like for a subject to undergo the relevant experience, and that what that experience is depends, somehow, on the state of one's body. However, the peripheric theory moves beyond those claims by identifying emotion with bodily feeling.

The notion of "bodily feeling" ranges over a wide variety of conscious phenomena and is thus significant in clarifying which, if any, of those phenomena should count as emotions. Bodily feelings fall into at least three different categories. We have localized sensations (such as pains, pangs or tingles), whereby consciousness is aware of a part of the body as being in a particular state. We have kinaesthetic awareness of parts of our body moving or standing in space. And we also have global feelings of how our body is overall (energetic, lethargic, "light" or a "burden").

Expressions of emotion are often followed by claims about how one feels overall, without one being expected to specify what, how or where exactly one feels what one feels. Hence, the last of the above-mentioned categories might look quite promising for identifying emotion with bodily feeling.[5] However, the promise draws on the vagueness that comes with the term "global feelings". One would wish for some details about the exact role of such feelings in emotional economy. After all, feeling sleepy or energetic is not an emotion, and nor is the global sensation of fatigue or exhaustion occasioned by physical exercise. If the peripheric theorist were to claim that these examples are too restrictive, and that the idea of "global feeling" is even broader than that, we may question the value of the proposed identification of emotion with such an accommodating, and rather elusive, candidate. Finally, the elusiveness of the idea of "how one feels overall" invites the rejoinder that it need not involve the body at all. Talk of global feelings might simply be another way of talking about our strongly held beliefs or evaluative judgements about what matters greatly to us.

A more promising way to effect the identification of emotion with bodily feeling is through the awareness of alterations in particular areas of the body, such as changes in skin temperature or electric conductiveness, and in the muscular, vascular, visceral and respiratory systems. Peripheric theorists assert, and their opponents deny, that emotion is identical to the perception of (a cluster of) patterned bodily changes. Their disagreement often spins into an exchange of counter-examples to the position advanced by each party. A positive side effect of this situation, that goes largely unnoticed, is the sharpening of our awareness of the phenomenology of emotional experience. A rather unwelcome consequence, though, is that raising doubts about one side of the argument can be mistaken for an outright rejection of a whole approach to emotions. Sartre's remarks on peripheric theory are a case in point. Having stated his objections to certain aspects of that theory, Sartre moves on to examine accounts that place little emphasis on the bodily dimension of emotional phenomena. It may thus be thought that Sartre belongs in the line of philosophers who reject peripheric theory because that theory attaches emotion to the body. However, that is not what a reading of Sartre's text allows us to infer. Sartre's objection is not that the theory lets the body in, but that it leaves the meaning out. To understand this view, I shall reconstruct the dialectic between the peripheric theorist and his opponent, with a view to illuminate the Sartrean take on this debate.

VI

An opening move in the debate is made by the objection that the identification of emotion with bodily feeling does not allow for a distinction between emotions that are clearly different. Consider emotions that are intimately related to the sense of ownership or accountability for our attitudes. Guilt is felt when I commit a moral transgression, shame when a negative image of myself has been publicly projected; the former denotes an action that ought (not) to have been performed, the latter an exposed character failure. Yet, despite their essential difference, the two emotions might bodily feel the same – and not only to each other, but also to a number of other emotional events, such as embarrassment, regret or remorse.

One might respond to this objection by claiming that although there are bodily differences between the above-mentioned emotions, we happen not to be able to experience any. However, this is not a viable response for the peripheric theorist, who purports to match emotion with the feeling of bodily changes as they occur, that is, of changes that are directly discernible by consciousness. Note that this problem remains even if we were to invoke an "as-if loop" of brain events that bypass the body.[6] That hypothesis postulates brain mechanisms that anticipate or simulate bodily changes, speeding up the organism's response to a situation, in the absence of any bodily perturbations. However, that hypothesis purports to retain the reality of feeling, by cancelling its veridical status: emotion is thus equated with the hallucinatory perception of (non-existent) bodily changes. Whatever the plausibility of that hypothesis, it does not – nor, I think, does it intend to – offer a solution to the problem of telling apart emotions with identical bodily outlook. If shame, guilt, embarrassment and other emotions come with the same bodily experience, then the peripheric theorist should endorse the counter-intuitive claim that these emotions are not just related, but are actually the same. If the theorist maintains that the emotions are different despite their common bodily outlook, then he should concede that it is not the bodily feeling that identifies an emotion for what it is, and that sets it apart from other emotions.

As neither horn of the dilemma is particularly attractive, the peripheric theorist might fall back on the claim that, despite initial appearances, the emotions of guilt, shame, embarrassment and so on do come with some subtly different bodily sensations. However, even if that were so, and if, for instance, our respiratory or vascular state in guilt is different from that in embarrassment, it is very doubtful that it is on the basis of such differences that we distinguish one emotion from the other. In answering the question of what one feels in a particular situation, one engages with one's relation to the salient facts of the case. For example, if a student is not feeling guilty for cheating in an exam, but feeling embarrassed for being caught, we would not expect him to confirm whether it is guilt or embarrassment that he is experiencing by checking his pulse rate.

The peripheric theorist might respond by drawing on evidence from the neurobiological, anthropological and behavioural sciences to the effect that there are emotions that come with a distinctive bodily outlook. The sharp differences in their physiological aspects allows for a clear distinction between those emotions. The problem with this response is that even if we were to take that evidence at face value – and it is not clear that we should – the evidence speaks to only a few human emotions (to five, possibly six, basic emotions, depending on the theory one holds).[7] Hence, the theory leaves dozens of emotions unaccounted for.

There are two ways for the somatic theorist to proceed at this point. He may provide a reductive analysis that breaks down each non-basic emotion to a combination of some or all of the basic ones. Or he may keep the number of possible bodily feelings limited, but introduce a range of evaluations as the ingredient that, added to a particular bodily awareness, may produce a large number of different emotions. The latter move signals a retreat from the somatic theory project, at least in its original form. The appeal to evaluation as the determining factor in the identity of emotions entails that talk about bodily feelings gives us only part of the story, and not the most interesting one.

This leaves the reductionist model as the only candidate for mapping emotions to (a combination of) bodily feelings. However, the model is subject to the charge of irrelevance; even if the bodily changes occurring in feeling jealous are a synthesis of all the bodily changes occurring in feeling angry, sad, disgusted and afraid, it is not on the basis of being (positionally) aware of such bodily changes that one is (non-positionally) aware of feeling jealous. Rather, it is by focusing on the manifest features of the world – the smirk on the other's face, the lameness of her excuses – that one is attributing betrayal to the other, and jealousy to oneself. If jealousy should be identified with perception it would be the perception of her dismissive gesture, not of the change in the location of your diaphragm.

The distinction between the two types of awareness shows the force and the subtlety of – what I consider to be – the Sartrean critique. Sartre's complaint is not that, for example, in feeling jealous one is not undergoing any bodily processes; his criticism is that when one is focusing on the physiological processes associated with an emotion, one finds something more and something other than such processes (*STE* 16). One finds something more because, however much information one accumulates about the mechanics of bodily events, one is none the wiser as to which, if any, of the emotions these events pick out in the absence of any information of how the agent perceives, evaluates or responds to the salient features of a situation. And one finds something other because, however much a bodily state is perturbed in an emotional occurrence, the physiological disturbance cannot account for the disturbing character of emotional experience. The point applies even to intense emotions such as terror, whereby one's body is set in a distinctive pattern (pulse changing, muscles tensed and the whole body "freezing"). Any such change, looked at for what it is, may indicate medical risks or benefits for the well-being of the organism, but it cannot account for the atrocious character of a terrorized consciousness. And part of the explanation for the discrepancy between a (positional) awareness of pulse rate, and a (non-positional) awareness of terror is that the former is exhausted by the perception of modifications in one's body, while the latter denotes a "relation between our psychic being and the world". That relation is not an arbitrary product of "quantitative, continuous modifications of vegetative states" (*STE* 15), but the realization of an "organised and describable structure" that involves the human being in situation (*STE* 17).

The peripheric theory locates emotion on the inner side of bodily experience, at the cost of leaving the agent's relation to the world outside the theory's purview. Cut off from the rest of reality, emotion becomes the self-enclosed, private, "internal" affair of someone who is subject to bodily perturbations. Emotion is thus deprived of its significance: the theory accounts neither for what the emotion indicates for the life of the person who is angry, jealous or joyous, nor for what his anger, jealousy or joy is really about.

VII

It appears that the culprit for the failure of peripheric theory is the emphasis on the awareness of physiological events. It is thus reasonable to look outside the domain of physiological changes for an alternative account of emotional phenomena. The second theory examined by Sartre focuses on the behavioural manifestations of emotional experience. The theory leaves behind the private chambers of bodily sensations for the public space of human interaction.

The theory under consideration purports to analyse emotion in terms of the behaviour exhibited by a subject in the grip of an emotion.[8] Sartre introduces that approach as a corrective to the peripheric theory's preoccupation with inward feelings, and he spends some time illustrating the approach with specific examples that give additional plausibility to the behaviourist reading of emotional reactions. This can give the impression that Sartre's own theory is identical to, or, at best, an elaboration on, the behaviourist paradigm. However, that impression is misleading. Given that several of the criticisms directed against the Sartrean theory are driven by this impression, it is important to clarify why and to what extent Sartre is attracted to certain aspects of the behaviourist theory.

We may identify three features of that theory that appeal to Sartre. It is a theory that views emotion as an integral part of a subject's interaction with her environment, it purports to highlight aspects of emotional phenomena that are amenable to objective description, and it offers a method of understanding the occurrence of emotional reactions that might otherwise appear unnecessary or counterproductive (*STE* 18). The last point is the most significant for our discussion. I shall reconstruct the analysis of emotional behaviour offered by the present model before addressing some theoretical and methodological questions about the Sartrean interpretation of behaviourism.

A subject encounters a situation that calls for a certain type of action, A1. What makes the performance of A1 the appropriate type of response is determined by the goal the subject is to achieve, in the light of her particular role, as this is set by the implicit or explicit (cultural, social, family, etc.) rules that – ought to – govern her behaviour in the relevant context. However, in some circumstances the cost of performing A1 is too much for the subject to incur. She therefore opts for a different response, A2, whose enactment transforms the shape of the situation in a way that the subject is released from the obligation of performing A1. Because A2 falls short of achieving the declared goal, it signals a kind of failure or "defeat" on the part of the subject. That behaviour of defeat is the emotion (*STE* 19).

The above paragraph outlines the sequence of events that, according to the theory under consideration, constitute an emotional episode. However, what makes that theory of emotion behaviourist is not its analysis of emotion in terms of that sequence, but the particular way that sequence is interpreted. The behaviourist understands that sequence as a continuous process that leads seamlessly from the presentation of a demand to the subject to the subject's responding in a sub-optimal fashion. The mechanics of that response is a focal point of discussion within the behaviourist school of thought. One can invoke the existence of nervous or psychic energy that is discharged according to the mechanical law of least resistance. Which action is performed is a matter of which channel is followed by the nervous energy that governs one's organic and bodily processes. Opting for one response over another is thus explained as the "switching of the liberated nervous energy on to another line" (*STE* 18; cf. 19, 21). Alternatively one can appeal to the activity of biologically grounded reflexes. When the sophisticated patterns of behaviour developed in adult life fail to meet the demands generated by threatening or otherwise troublesome situations, we automatically revert to a response set off by the nerve circuit that conditioned our reactions at the early stages of our development. Locating the source of emotion in the "primitive circuit" of reflex behaviour operative in very early childhood allows the "pure behaviourist" to conceive of emotions as basic and universally valid modes of adaptation (*STE* 20). Contemporary neurobiological theories provide elaborate versions of this approach that identify basic emotions with a small set of reflex mechanisms. However the details of the relevant mechanism are filled out, the main point is that emotion constitutes a fall-back option for an organism when "all the ways are barred" and the going gets tough (*STE* 39).

The plausibility of this account can be challenged in a number of ways, some of which are less effective than others. We might claim that the account fails because it conceives of emotion as nothing but a matter of behaviour. This claim, though, amounts to the complaint that behaviourism about emotion is false because it is behaviourist. And although one might have independent grounds for rejecting behaviourism *tout court*, it is not, in this context, the more fruitful way to proceed. Sartre, for one, avoids such a wholesale attack, arguing instead that behaviourism fails to deliver on its promise of restoring the reality of emotional phenomena by looking beyond the narrow confines of bodily perturbations, at the meaning of our transactions with the world. For those transactions to be meaningful two criteria should be met.

The first is that the emotional transaction should be an adaptation of the organism to the situation. If this condition is to be met, then the organism should be aware of the behaviour conducive to the declared goal, the difficulties involved in behaving that way, the availability of adopting an alternative behaviour, and the opting for that alternative as a (in a sense sub-optimal, but nevertheless functional) way out of an impasse. Hence, the occurrence of the alternative behaviour should be something other than a mechanical process of switching nervous energy channels.

Thus, the second criterion is that the account should not leave behaviour proper out of its picture. Discharged nervous energy is not just sub-optimal behaviour; rather, it is no behaviour at all. Analysing emotive behaviour as a set of arbitrary organic diffusions "would be less like a behaviour of defeat than a lack of behaviour" (*STE* 19).

In my reading, Sartre's main argument against behaviourism is that it fails on its own terms. Moreover, behaviourism does not enable us to distinguish the reasons behind the occurrence of different patterns of emotional reaction when several of those reactions (frustration, fear, amusement, rage or intimidation) can very well be triggered in different individuals or in the same individuals at different times, by exactly the same remark. Finally, it does not sufficiently distinguish between emotions, on the one hand, and phenomena that can more easily be seen as the outcome of automatic nervous switches, such as emotional shock or nervous crises, on the other (*STE* 21).

Note, though, that analogous problems are faced by the functionalist account, propounded by Gestalt psychology, and partly endorsed by Sartre (*STE* 27). Emotional reaction is here interpreted as an abrupt solution to a problem, whereby the prescribed form of behaviour is substituted by behaviour that cancels the demands made on the subject through changing the shape of her situation. However, the mere affirmation of the occurrence of a form of behaviour does not amount to an explanation of that occurrence. If the explanation is to be sought in the end brought about by the occurrence, then an account is owed of how and why a particular end calls for, and brings forth, a particular form of behaviour. What we are offered, instead, is the description of the break-up of one form of behaviour followed by the reconstitution of another form of behaviour. The result is an account of a succession of forms that sounds true but incomprehensible. The missing ingredient, according to Sartre, is an explication of the meaning of the forms that, according to Gestalt theorists, constitute an emotion.[9]

All in all, behaviourism – old and new – fails to interpret emotion as a meaningful aspect of our being in the world. Yet, that criticism is not by itself very helpful in the absence of an account of what makes something meaningful. I suggest that for Sartre emotion is meaningful because it is a conscious adaptation of the agent to her situation. The exact nature of adaptation involved in an emotional episode will be discussed in the final section of the chapter. Before that, though, we should examine the Sartrean claim that it is consciousness that makes emotion meaningful. Is it not possible that emotions acquire their significance through a process from which consciousness is absent? Are there not unconscious emotions?

VIII

Talk of the unconscious in the philosophy of emotions refers mainly to two things. It can denote an emotion whose existence is not in any way present to consciousness (Freud 1953–74: vol. I, 260). Or, it can refer to emotional phenomena whose meaning lies in the unconscious (*ibid.*: vol. XIV, 167). It is the latter issue that occupies Sartre in the *Sketch*. Although his philosophy is inhospitable to unconscious states in general, it is important not to mistake his critique of the psychoanalytic view of emotions, for a wholesale attack on the idea of an unconscious mind.[10] Before we look at Sartre's critique, let me outline the psychoanalytic approach to emotions.[11]

Psychoanalysis consists in a therapeutic practice, and a set of theoretical claims and methodological principles that ground and inform the practice. In the therapeutic context, the analyst purports to help the analysand understand various aspects of her life that are a source of concern to her, and that seem to resist a simple interpretation. The process of interpretation requires that the analyst attribute to the analysand various states of which the analysand is unaware. The analytical process is based on the premises that the analysand's experience means something, and that what it means may not be apparent to the analysand herself. For instance, the subject might relate to the analyst an incident in which she behaved in a way for which she can provide no reason, at least none that would satisfy a reasonable interpreter of that incident, including herself during the therapeutic session. By drawing on material presented by the subject (through linguistic and non-verbal communication) during the therapeutic sessions, the analyst weaves together a story that can account for the otherwise inexplicable behaviour.

The possible reactions of the analysand to the interpretation offered by the analyst are not presently a concern for our discussion.[12] What is important is that the analyst purports to articulate an interpretation of what is said by the subject, filling gaps in her talk and drawing connections that tie up seemingly unrelated points in a way that enables us to make sense of the analysand's experience.

Classical psychoanalysis asserts that the interpretation of emotional phenomena should postulate mental items that are absent from the analysand's consciousness. These items are primarily motivational states (such as instincts, drives or desires) that have been repressed at an early stage of the subject's psychological development. Repression is the process by which certain states are thrown into the unconscious, and are kept there. However, their life in hiding is not without consequence: the states are unconscious but active (Freud 1953–74: vol. XII, 261). Their activity consists in the production of behaviour that expresses the repressed desires.

The therapeutic benefits of the psychoanalytic practice are to a large extend dependent on the breadth and accuracy of the interpretations articulated in the analytic sessions. The importance of interpretations generated during that process is not questioned by Sartre. What he is questioning is the validity of the meta-psychological interpretation of the practice, propounded by classical psychoanalysis.[13]

As Sartre understands it, psychoanalytic theory dissociates the phenomenon analysed from its signification. What the phenomenon signifies is the repressed state that, unbeknown to the subject, produces the behaviour under consideration. The relation between the behaviour and its signification is supposed to be that between an effect and its cause. The former depends on the latter for its production, but, like all causally related items, they are distinct things that may exist separately from each other, and, thus, acquaintance with the one does not entail knowledge of the other (*STE* 31). The wet pavement is the outcome of events that involve dark clouds, yet a totally inexperienced observer cannot "read" the clouds by looking at the wet paving stones. In fact, the whole idea of "reading" or "interpreting" clouds in the pavement does not make much sense. A better characterization would be that of explaining the process by which an event was brought about by its cause.

Psychoanalysis postulates a similar connection between conscious behaviour and its unconscious grounds. It is claimed that the repressed desire that causes the behaviour lies outside the domain of conscious engagement with the world. As the mechanical product of psychic causality, conscious conduct passively receives its identity from something external to it. Accordingly, an examination of how an agent experiences a situation and of how she responds to it will not enable us to understand her behaviour without invoking a meta-theory of causal connections that designates fixed relations between the events under consideration and their alleged sources.[14]

Whatever the metaphysical credentials of a theory of psychic causality, the problem is that it undermines the very practice that it is supposed to sustain. Viewing human conduct as passively produced by forces that lie outside the domain of meaningful activity, and which are only externally related to that conduct, is in clear tension with the analytic practice of looking into the particular features and context of a situation (as all these are conveyed by the analysand's communication) in order to interpret her behaviour: in order to understand what it means. And it is precisely this tension, between the practitioner's search for meaning and the theoreticians' postulation of fixed causal relations, that erodes the foundations of the psychoanalytic approach to emotions: "The profound contradiction in all psychoanalysis is that it presents at the same time a bond of causality and a bond of understanding between the phenomena that it studies. These two types of relationship are incompatible" (*STE* 32–3).

It is worth pausing for a moment to consider the exact nature of the Sartrean critique of the psychoanalytic view of emotional phenomena. One might argue that the psychoanalytic approach is grounded on the idea of an unconscious mind, but as no such mind exists, the approach is incorrect. That is not the way Sartre argues in the present context; and this is all to the good for two reasons. First, the proposed argument begs the question against psychoanalysis by presupposing, rather than trying to establish, that the appeal to the unconscious is deeply problematic. Second, the idea of "an unconscious mind" is usually taken to imply that we are hosts of two minds, one conscious and one unconscious. That view, however, is rejected even by psychoanalysts. According to some classical discussions of this issue, "the unconscious" is not the name of some mental entity, but an adjective that characterizes various states or processes to which consciousness is denied access.[15] Whether or not the latter view of the unconscious is itself plausible, the point remains that the Sartrean critique does not invoke assumptions denied by its opponent.

Another way one might object to the psychoanalytic approach would be to claim that, even if the idea of the unconscious could prove useful in other domains, the nature of emotional experience is such that it renders implausible any denial of the subject's ability to tell what her own experience really means. However, that is not a claim to which Sartre subscribes. Casting doubts about the unconscious need not be followed by a declaration of mental transparency. Sartre only asserts that the signification of an emotional phenomenon should be sought in our conscious engagement with the world. This does not mean that "the signification must be perfectly explicit. There are many possible degrees of condensation and of clarity" (*STE* 31–2).

Finally, I think that the Sartrean critique respects the important distinction between the preconscious and the unconscious. Preconscious is a state that is not currently conscious either because consciousness is occupied with matters unrelated to that state, or because the state is relevant to present circumstances, but, for various reasons, is kept out of conscious awareness. In some cases, the analytic process brings a preconscious state into the foreground, by offering a name to a state that was up to that point unidentified by the analysand, acknowledging its existence, and the role it plays in her behaviour.[16] The recognition of the state is possible because, according to the psychoanalytic story, the preconscious state (as opposed to an unconscious state) is never too far from consciousness. Bringing the preconscious to consciousness is a matter of making explicit and occurrent what was latent and implicit. However, implicit awareness is still awareness, and a process of interpretation that focused just on preconscious states would be one that aimed to make the analysand own up to aspects of her life of which she was implicitly aware. This might be a perfectly legitimate process, but it is not the primary concern of psychoanalytic work. Psychoanalysis is mainly interested in states that transcend conscious awareness, because it is a theory premised on the view that "the signification of conscious behaviour lies wholly outside the behaviour itself", in the unconscious forces that supposedly cause that behaviour (*STE* 30).

We may see now that Sartre's critique takes psychoanalysis on its own terms and points to an inconsistency inherent in its theoretical system. His main argument is to the effect that the theory of the unconscious causation is in conflict with the practice of analysis. The practice aims at understanding by means of interpreting the meaning of the analysand's behaviour. The theory sees behaviour as the causal outcome of processes that lie outside behaviour itself; indeed, the story goes, if the source of behaviour were not outside one's consciousness then one would claim no difficulty in understanding what her behaviour means (Freud 1953–74: vol. XIV, 169). By separating behaviour from its signification, the theory cancels the analytical project of making sense of human conduct by attending to the meanings communicated by the analysand.

A defender of classical psychoanalysis might retort that Sartre's argumentation is inconclusive. At most, it puts forward a dilemma between (i) adopting a theory of psychic causality, and (ii) pursuing a practice of understanding the analysand by interpreting the meaning inherent in the structure of her conduct. The Sartrean critique might present us with a choice, but it cannot, as it stands, force us to abandon the metapsychological theory in favour of the analytical practice.

That is a fair objection, but it can be answered by placing Sartre's critique in its broader philosophical context. The rejection of psychoanalytic theory is grounded on the Sartrean view of consciousness. The theory of psychic causality entails that consciousness is a passive being, which acquires its identity and signification from things external to itself. However, according to Sartre, consciousness is not some spiritual or material thing: it is awareness of things. Conscious activity, in perception, thinking and action, is (non-positionally) aware of itself being (positionally) engaged with the world. However, if the psychoanalytic theory is true, then consciousness, being a product of forces to which it is unrelated, can very well be unaware of itself being awareness of whatever it is conscious of. And that, according to Sartre, is a contradiction in terms (*STE* 31, 33).

IX

Emotional behaviour cannot be interpreted satisfactorily by an appeal to unconscious causes, not so much because they are unconscious, but because they are causes. However, this leaves open the question of whether emotions themselves can be unconscious. We shall address this question by looking at the two sources of pressure against the Sartrean view of consciousness as a necessary aspect of emotional experience. The first comes from classical psychoanalysis, and the second from contemporary work in cognitive psychology. Let us consider each account in turn.

One can build a case for the possibility of unconscious emotions by trying to extend the psychoanalytic view of the unconscious so as to include emotional states. Let us assume that there is no *a priori* stricture on what can fall in the category of the unconscious. What makes something unconscious is the process of repression by which that thing moves out of conscious awareness and is kept there. Given the psychological power of intense or recalcitrant emotions, it is only natural to think that emotions would be among the primary targets of repression.[17] Ordinary experience seems to lend support to this view. We often encounter a friend who would deny that she experiences an emotion (such as anger, jealousy or sadness) that, it is obvious to us, suffuses every waking moment of her life. A simple explanation of that phenomenon would be that although the emotion is present in that person's experience, it is absent from her consciousness; in other words, it is an unconscious emotion.

This might look like an attractive proposal for introducing unconscious emotions, but it faces several problems. Psychoanalysis conceives of mental states in terms of thought contents, or of affects, or, as in the case of emotions, of combinations of mental content and affect.[18] The process of repression effects a dissociation of the thought from the affective energy originally attached to its content. Hence, the thought is kept in the unconscious and the affect either dissipates or acquires a different form, ranging from free-floating anxiety to the sophisticated activities of artistic creation. Consequently we can no longer speak of an emotion being (in the) unconscious. What we can say at the most is that a constituent of it, namely its thought content, is kept beyond conscious awareness.

At this point, theorists who identify emotion by its thought component could argue that admitting the existence of repressed thoughts amounts to an acceptance of unconscious emotions. If all that characterizes an emotion essentially is the thought (cognition, or judgement) that something befalls a person, a quality or an object that is of import to one's wellbeing, and that thought remains inaccessible to consciousness, then we should conclude that there are unconscious emotions.[19]

For this argument to succeed, one would have to accept that a conscious thought retains its identity after it has been repressed. However, human thoughts are not little rocks that survive through much movement. The identity of a thought is a matter of the constancy of its content in reasoning, reflection or deliberation. What a thought is depends to a large extent on how it is related to other thoughts one has, and of how the whole network of thoughts is structured into interrelated units of meaningful content. And the problem with the cognitivist manoeuvre is that the norms that govern conscious thought – most notably the principle of non-contradiction, the rules of temporary succession, and the distinction between the internal and the external – do not (allegedly) apply to the realm of unconscious processes. Therefore, the relations of entailment, implication or negation that characterize the content of a thought do not necessarily carry through to the unconscious. A thought entertained yesterday with a content that implied *p*, and a thought occurring today with a content implying not-*p*, is not *ceteris paribus* the same thought. It is therefore not clear what sense can be made of the idea that thoughts repressed in the unconscious are identical to their conscious predecessors. But if that idea is implausible, so is the idea that emotions, reduced to their thought component, can move to the unconscious without losing their identity.

One way of rescuing the cognitivist scenario would be to claim that it is plausible to see the emotion-thought through its transformations so that, if and when it comes to the surface at an analytic session, one is able to identify it as an up-to-that-point unconscious emotion. However, keeping track of the transformations of a mental state implies that the state is within the purview of consciousness, and thus that it is not unconscious.

The failure of what I have called the cognitivist appropriation of the psychoanalytic view of unconscious states is symptomatic of the problems that beset the interpretation of the unconscious as a second mind, populated by contentful states that just happen to inhabit a mental universe that runs in parallel to the conscious one. What the correct interpretation of the unconscious might be is an issue that far exceeds the scope of this book.

I have argued that neither the classical treatment of these issues, nor its cognitivist versions, can establish the reality of unconscious emotions. Let me now turn to the discussion of relevant research in contemporary psychology.

X

An evaluation of recent work in experimental psychology would be facilitated by understanding what exactly the issue is that the work purports to explore. However, a careful reading of the relevant literature reveals that there are several different meanings attributed to the locution "unconscious emotion", with the result that the debating parties may talk past each other. I suggest that we adopt the meaning attributed by psychologists, who argue in favour of the existence of unconscious emotion. In that way, we offer the opposition a fair hearing, allowing for the possibility that the claim for the necessary presence of consciousness in emotional phenomena should be qualified or even abandoned in the light of the relevant evidence. We can capture the sense in which emotion can be unconscious in attributing to someone the experience of an emotion of which she is not aware. With that in mind, let us look at the evidence submitted in favour of unconscious emotions.

Unconscious emotions have been thought to underpin the phenomenon of alexithymia.[20] Subjects are characterized as alexithymics when they systematically show difficulty in identifying or describing their own emotions. The sources of that phenomenon are a matter of debate among cognitive psychologists and neuropsychologists.[21] However, what is not in dispute is that the subjects experience emotions and, in most cases, are also able to report on that experience. What they lack is an ability to place their emotion under some set category, or to identify the causes of their experience.[22] Lacking that ability may limit the range of their affective responses, as well as hinder the development of personal attachments enabled by communicating or sharing our emotional experience. None of these points, though, tell against the view that the subjects are not unconscious of their emotional experience. To oppose that view one would have to establish that the subject is not aware of her experience unless, first, she knows what caused the experience, and second, she is able to conceptualize and express in linguistic medium the nature of that experience. Both assumptions are highly controversial and there are reasons to cast doubt on their plausibility. There are several of our experiences we would find hard to describe, but we do not take this difficulty as a reason for denying their existence. Moreover, we may feel puzzled about what really caused the way we currently feel, but, again, we do not treat this as a ground for denying that we are feeling something. Alexithymia shows how sharp these difficulties might become in extreme circumstances; it usually follows traumatic experiences that, we may assume, the subject would not to want to process conceptually, to describe and categorize (Lane *et al.* 1997). Conscious experience is not necessarily conceptually structured and linguistically packaged. Therefore, the difficulty to conceptualize and talk about one's emotional experience provides, as such, no evidence against the view that one is conscious of the experience.

XI

I have belaboured this point because it will prove useful in the discussion of the next, and perhaps major, case presented by defenders of unconscious emotions. So-called "fear conditioning"[23] refers to experiments where subjects are exposed for a very short period of time to stimuli that can be received as a danger to the subjects, who then exhibit physiological changes, such as increased electrical conductance of the skin (skin conductance), which are also characteristic of experiencing fear.[24] We have two main variations on this theme. In some experiments, a neutral stimulus appears simultaneously with a mild electric shock or other unpleasant event; in other studies, images of things that have been treated as dangerous by the subjects, such as snakes or spiders, are projected masked by neutral stimuli for a period of time that is too short for processing the relevant images conceptually.[25] In both cases, the reappearance of the neutral stimulus in the subject's vicinity is followed by autonomic changes, and facial or bodily alterations that are similar to phenomena exhibited in fear response. The moral drawn from such cases is that the subjects, unbeknown to themselves, are experiencing fear. Is that conclusion justified?

We may answer this question by considering the dialectic of the arguments for and against the possibility of unconscious fear. It is assumed that the duration and manner of exposure to the stimuli precludes the possibility of processing the relevant information in a way that permits the formation of an appraisal of the stimuli. It is further assumed that such an appraisal is necessary for the experience to be conscious. Both assumptions reflect the standard interpretation of ordinary cases where someone can account for her experience (of fear) by pointing to the things she perceives (as dangerous). Let us grant that those assumptions are in order when we wish to understand the subject's account of her emotional experience. However, is offering an account of the experience necessary for an experience to be conscious? The fact that someone cannot tell why she feels fear might imply all sorts of unwelcome things about her situation, but it does not entail that she is not aware of being afraid.

It is worth noting here that, in ordinary discourse, denials of understanding why one feels a particular emotion are often a means of highlighting one's own dissatisfaction with what appears to be the cause of the emotion. Usually, it is not a matter of not being able to refer to anything at all as a cause for one's feelings, but that none of the obvious candidates seems to satisfy one's quest for the real cause. However, my response to the argument from fear conditioning does not depend on such a loose reading of "I don't know why I feel like that all day". My point is that conscious experience does not require awareness of the causes of that experience.

A proponent of unconscious emotions might retort that it is not only the causes of the emotion that are unconscious; it is the emotion itself. The assumption here is that it sounds totally improbable to claim that a subject can be aware of experiencing fear in the span of milliseconds within which the exposure to stimuli lasts. That claim is indeed implausible, but admitting its implausibility lands the defender of unconscious emotions with a dilemma, neither horn of which is very attractive.

First, we may deny that the subject is able to be conscious of experiencing fear in a span of milliseconds for the simple reason that no such experience can occur in a span of milliseconds. Thus we can accept that no awareness of fear occurs by admitting that there was no fear to be aware of in the first place. However, by accepting this, the whole case for unconscious emotion is thrown away.

The second horn of the dilemma states that we should believe in the existence of the emotion on grounds other than those already dismissed, that is, awareness of the causes of the emotion, or awareness of the emotion itself. What grounds? The obvious answer is the occurrence of physiological changes that follow on stimuli exposure, such as skin conductance and other autonomic changes. It is usually taken for granted that such changes should count as "fear response". However, far from being self-evident, it is precisely this point that needs most support from the defender of unconscious emotions. It is not clear why changes in skin conductance, say, amount to an emotional response in the absence of any other relevant considerations. Raised hair on your skin is a response, but it is not by itself a "fear" response: perhaps your woollen jumper is too rough, or your back is exposed to a mild draught.[26]

To see how this has a bearing on the current problem, consider first the case where such changes (owing to their extremely short life span or because one's mind is otherwise occupied) are not in any way registered by the subject. The subject is in a safe place, and is not aware of any change in her body, or in her environment, or in her thinking. Does it still make sense to talk about that subject as experiencing fear? I believe not.

Consider, on the other hand, the case where the subject is aware of her raising skin hair. We may then assert that she has a feeling of a change located in her body. However, a bodily feeling does not on its own an emotional feeling make.[27] In either case, we have not been offered an argument that would establish that the occurrence of physiological alterations induced in an experimental setting amounts to emotional experience.

I have argued that a critical examination of the relevant theoretical work in psychoanalytic and experimental psychology casts serious doubt on the reality of unconscious phenomena. Whether some alternative interpretation of the phenomena can resuscitate the belief in unconscious emotions is an important issue that should have a bearing on not only the interpretation of the Sartre's theory, but also on our explanation, interpretation and evaluation of human emotions.

XII

The positive account offered by Sartre is articulated through a dialectical process of considering, rebutting and moving beyond the constraints of various preconceptions about emotional phenomena. Let us take stock of this process.

The standard way of thinking about emotions is as a type of psychic state. Sartre argues that states are the product of a reflexive act directed towards a range of past experiences of feeling, thinking and acting. In a reversal of actual priorities, the feelings, thoughts or actions that constitute the lived experience are considered to have their source in fixed psychic entities that guide one's stance towards the world. Giving lived experience its due is the first task of a phenomenological theory of emotion. A classic proposal on how to understand emotional experience is to reduce emotion as a whole to a particular type of feeling, namely, to awareness of bodily changes. We have seen that the reductivist project fails: looking at emotional experience we always find something more and something else than awareness of our bodily condition. However, that attempt rightly emphasized the role of the body in emotional experience, so Sartre moves on to consider an alternative way of making sense of emotion as embodied phenomenon: emotion understood through its role in engendering behaviour that, in some way, releases the subject from the constraints of a demanding situation. Sartre is very sympathetic to this approach, but he is questioning its ability to make sense of the agent's emotional engagement with reality. In particular, the approach allows for the possibility of emotional behaviour taking place in the total absence of the agent's consciousness of the world and of her stance towards it. I argued that this move is highly problematic. On the one hand, as Sartre shows, the attempt to interpret the meaning of emotional behaviour in terms of unconscious forces is based on a serious confusion between reasons and causes. On the other hand, the evidence supplied by cognitive and experimental psychology, when carefully examined, is too thin to justify a belief in the alleged existence of unconscious emotions. All in all, this leaves the conscious engagement with reality as the only field where emotional experience unfolds.

The critique of the standard approaches to emotion paves the way for a positive account of emotional phenomena. A common way of presenting Sartre's own view is with the catchphrase "emotions are actions" (see e.g. Neu 2000: ch. 1). The phrase expresses the metaphysical claim that emotion itself is a type of event that falls under the category of action. In the present section I shall show that this way of reading Sartre is incorrect.

The core of the Sartrean view is that during an emotional episode one's relation to the world is "magically" transformed by means of one's body (*STE* 39–41). Let me explicate what that means. The world is understood as a totality of phenomena linked by a complex network of references to each other. The way in which each phenomenon relates to others defines the type of world encountered by the subject. In the world of daily activity, we experience reality as a combination of demands (for projects awaiting completion, bills to be paid, walls to be decorated) and affordances (given by fast computers, bank transfers, or DIY shops). The link between demands and affordances is itself experienced as ruled by deterministic processes between causes and effects. The "instrumental world" of action is captured in the "pragmatic intuition" of the situation that makes certain moves available for the subject, while denying her others (*STE* 39). And this points to a major contrast between action and emotion: for Sartre the world encountered in emotional experience – what we variously characterize as a "hateful", "joyful" or "bleak" world – far from being identical to the world of action, is clearly distinguished from the instrumental world (*STE* 35). The distinction here is twofold.

On the one hand, the "emotional apprehension" of the world hooks on to those qualities or aspects that carry affective meaning for the agent, while the "pragmatic intuition" focuses on features of the situation that make possible, or impossible, the execution of a task, the realization of an objective or the creation of a product.[28] On the other hand, the agent's response in an emotional episode engages the overall stance and physiology of the body not so as to effect material changes in the world, but so as to alter her perception of reality, and, through that, her relation to the world: "during emotion, it is the body which, directed by the consciousness, changes its relationship to the world so that the world should change its qualities" (*STE* 41). Sartre calls that change in qualities "magical" (*STE* 30, 43, 59). What makes the transformation of the world magical is that what changes is not the material constitution of reality but how reality appears to the agent and, consequently, how the agent responds to a thus transformed reality. That notion of "magical transformation" has, in my view, nothing mystifying about it: when Sartre talks about magic, in the present context, he appeals to the ordinary contrast between two ways in which things may change: *either* as abiding by, *or* as supposedly bypassing, and superseding, the deterministic processes that govern the normal run of events in the world.[29]

XIII

The notion of "emotional response" may also be variously interpreted, and it would help our discussion to attempt a clarification of the various meanings of the term. We may call a response "emotional" simply in order to distinguish it from other types of response: in pure thought, in imagination, or in practical deliberation whose aim is the achievement, through action, of a particular goal (*STE* 35). Second, we may interpret someone's overall stance or conduct towards a situation as (part of) her emotional response, when that stance or conduct symbolizes her emotion (*STE* 32). Unfortunately the notion of "symbolizing" is not itself unambiguous, and Sartre expends no time in clarifying it. I would suggest that the relevant sense is that of one thing (stance or conduct) communicating to a competent observer the presence of another thing (emotion) by being part of a larger whole containing the thing "symbolized".

This notion of symbolization seems to be operative in the Sartrean analysis of both "passive" emotions (as when one's bowed head and bent posture symbolizes one's sadness), and in the case of "active" emotions (as when one's shouting symbolizes one's rage). The whole that includes both the sadness and the physical listlessness, both the rage and the shouting, is the human being in a situation ("l'homme en situation"; *ETE* 27). However, according to Sartre, the holding of a relation between the symbolizing stance, attitude or conduct and the emotion symbolized is not some inexplicable fact of the universe, but is itself subject to further philosophical analysis. And the analysis propounded by Sartre highlights the functional character of emotional response, not only in the case of "active emotions" (as when one's shouting reduces the chances of properly listening to what anyone else says), but also in the case of "passive" emotions (as when one's bowed head and bent posture limits the range of one's vision, so that as little as possible of the cruel world is taken in).

Finally, there is a notion of "emotional response" that attaches to action that, while it can be described independently of the occurrence of emotion, is thought to be somehow better accounted for by reference to the emotion preceding the particular action. The issue here is quite tricky because strong but opposing intuitions seem to pull the analysis of this kind of "emotional response" in very different directions.[30] Let us distinguish among the following scenarios of running away from a dangerous-looking bear. Case 1 is where the agent weighs her options and, after relevant deliberation, decides to create quickly a sufficient distance between herself and the bear. Case 2 is as in the previous scenario, but with the emotion of fear preceding the thought process and action process described in Case 1. Case 2 can be subdivided into Case 2(a), whereby the fear experienced and the resulting action are temporally successive but otherwise unconnected; and Case 2(b), whereby the fear causes the deliberating process that results in the relevant action. In Case 1, the running away is rationalized by reference to the thought process (usually taken to include the putting together of one's beliefs and desires) that aims to lead the agent out of danger. In Case 2(b), the running away is accounted for (at the level of explanation) and also rationalized (at the level of justification) by invoking the emotion of fear, because it is that emotion that initiates the relevant thought process and action process. However, none of the above cases satisfy Sartre's description of fleeing as an emotional response.

Case 1 is a non-starter in the present context because, on the one hand, it includes no reference to emotion and, on the other hand, it implies an analysis (in terms of reflective consideration and manipulation of one's own beliefs and desires) that is false to the phenomenology of normal human activity (which is a non-reflective, outward looking engagement with the objects, tools and tasks of a situation).[31] Case 2(b) offers a more interesting, and (subject to qualifications about the proper analysis of human action in general) arguably correct, account of the phenomena involved. What it presents, though, is an analysis not of emotional response but of prudential action, and the two types of event are markedly different. Running out of prudence is acting according to a plan; emotional fleeing, on the other hand, is a "magical behaviour which negates the dangerous object with one's whole body, by reversing the vectorial structure of the space we live in and suddenly creating a potential direction on the other side" (*STE* 43). It is not a case of reaching for shelter (as in prudential behaviour) but of forgetting or negating the threat. The dangerous object is the focal point of fear, and – unlike in the case of prudential action – the faster one runs (the louder one shouts, the further one withdraws), the more afraid (or angry, or sad) one feels.

The Sartrean analysis of emotion ranges over a wide variety of phenomena that could not be reviewed in this chapter, not least because several of his points are simply acute observations made in the course of his unique narration of human phenomena, for which there is no substitute for reading Sartre's text itself. In the next section I shall address a worry regarding the internal consistency of the Sartrean analysis of emotions. At present, I would like to sum up by drawing attention to some parts of the text that seem to corroborate our interpretation of the Sartrean approach to emotion.

First, behaviour on its own (including one's overall conduct or particular actions *vis-à-vis* a situation) forms an important and integral part of emotional phenomena but is not, and should not be conceived as, exhaustive of what an emotion really is for Sartre: "behaviour pure and simple is not emotion, any more than is the pure and simple awareness of that behaviour" (*STE* 48). Second, emotional experience cannot be dissociated from the body on pain of "falsity" of the professed emotion: "the physiological phenomena … represent the genuineness of the emotion, they are the phenomena of belief" (*STE* 50). Third, what the agent believes is not some reflective statement about her own thoughts or bodily processes, but the reality of the affective meanings that make up the object on which the emotion feeds:

> Consciousness does not limit itself to the projection of affective meanings upon the world around it: it lives the new world it has thereby constituted – lives it directly, commits itself to it, and suffers from the qualities that the concomitant behaviour has outlined. (*STE* 51)

XIV

Near the end of his monograph, Sartre gives a counter-example to his own theory: "the immediate reactions of horror and wonder that sometimes possess us when certain objects suddenly appear to us" is not explained by the theory of emotions so far presented (*STE* 51). That critical remark is followed by a diagnosis for the apparent failure of the theory to account for those cases (*STE* 55–7), and a proposal as to how we could accommodate them in a phenomenological theory of emotions (*STE* 57–61). That proposal, though, may strike someone as as being at a significant distance from the main path of argumentation unfolded in the *Sketch*. It has been claimed (i) that there are two lines of reasoning in the text, which (ii) are in conflict with each other, and (iii) with the latter line being clearly the most satisfactory of the two.[32]

It appears to me that the above interpretation is not necessitated by the textual evidence; the *Sketch* is open to at least one different reading that avoids attributing to Sartre a major inconsistency. Let me first state briefly where the alleged inconsistency lies, and why – in my view – if it did exist, it would be a major one. The alleged inconsistency lies in the difference between the ways in which "magic" figures in the analysis of emotion. In the main line of reasoning presented in the *Sketch*, emotional experience is explained in terms of magical behaviour, which purports to change one's situation not by effecting changes in the world, but by changing the meaning of the situation; the behaviour is "magical" because the agent, by means of his body, affects the way the situation is laid out before him, without acting on it. Hence, instead of engaging directly with the nuts and bolts of the case, he stands towards it as if "the relations between things and their potentialities were not governed by deterministic processes but by magic" (*STE* 40). That account is carefully articulated over the first twenty pages of Section III, which outlines a "phenomenological theory of emotion". In the last five pages of that section, though, Sartre talks of magic as something found in reality as such, since in horror, terror and wonder "it is the world that … reveals itself suddenly as a magical environments" (*STE* 57).

According to the interpretation we are discussing, this "new" view of magic, is "more satisfactory" than the previous account, since it fits better with ordinary experience, because it acknowledges that affective experience does not create, but "discloses" the world to us (see Richmond 2010: 153–5).

To assess those claims, it is worth noting, first, that the "new" view of emotion favoured by that interpretation is not really that new: the view that emotion is a way of apprehending qualities of the world is put forward at the very beginning of Section III. Indeed, the view that things may suddenly reveal themselves to us as "hateful, horrible, likeable, etc.", as well as the claim that emotions are nothing but ways of disclosing (*decouvrir*) the world, already appear in Sartre's early paper "Intentionality" (IHP). Therefore, if the line of reasoning developed in the last five pages of Section III were deeply at odds with the reasoning presented in the previous pages, we would not simply have a case of inconsistency in a particular section, but a case of an author who keeps changing his mind, putting forward conflicting accounts in his various texts, as well as within paragraphs of a single text; and that is one of the reasons why, earlier on, I maintained that if the alleged inconsistency existed, it would be a major one.

The other reason concerns the principle that, according to the interpretation at hand, underpins the alleged inconsistency. For any pair of an emotional state (such as "horror") and a worldly quality (such as "the horrible"), one might ask which comes first: is the state dependent on the quality, or is the latter dependent on the emotion? The interpretation we examine asserts that the difference among the two conflicting lines of reasoning in the *Sketch* lies in a reversal of the order of dependency between state and quality: whereas for the first line of reasoning emotional behaviour generates "magically" the corresponding qualities of the situation, for the second line of reasoning, a "magical" quality is the cause, rather than the effect, of the related emotion (Richmond 2010: 153).

I think that there is something amiss with the above claims as a purported rendering of Sartre's own approach to the relation between emotion and its intentional correlate. To be sure, Sartre's considered answer to the question of dependency will appear much later than the *Sketch*, mainly in his analysis of "the circuit of the self" in *Being and Nothingness*, whereby it is shown that how the world appears to the agent evaluatively is a function of the agent's "fundamental project", which is ultimately grounded not in features of being-in-itself, but in the original choice of the self on the part of being-for-itself (*BN* 127–9).

Returning to the *Sketch*, we may note the absence of any detailed engagement with the traditional debate over the priority between "the mind" and "the world". Contemporary philosophy might be exercised by the question of whether the mind spreads itself on a neutral universe, or, conversely, whether intrinsically valuable objects impinge on a passively receptive mind. As is well known, the terms of that question were first clearly set out in the seventeenth century, and acquired new impetus at the end of the twentieth century.[33] However, that is not how the discussion is set within Sartre's outline of a phenomenological theory of emotions. The world out of which an emotional event arises is not a neutral terrain of causal interactions: it is a network of meanings, social demands and practical affordances, that Sartre summarily calls "the instrumental world" (*STE* 34–8).[34] Hence, he writes that in the phenomenon of anger there is a "continuous passage from the non-reflective consciousness 'instrumental world' (action) to the non-reflective consciousness 'hateful world'" (*STE* 35; cf. *STE* 60).

If I read Sartre's main line of reasoning correctly, emotional consciousness does not create qualities *ex nihilo*, since the situation it finds itself in is already shaped with the qualities that make up the instrumentally meaningful reality: the emotional world, Sartre writes, "is a transformation of" the instrumental world (*STE* 35). Therefore, it would be erroneous to attribute to his main analysis the view that the emotion "causes" value qualities, and then to contrast that view with a new theory according to which the value quality "causes" the emotion.

Nevertheless, when it comes to the issue of "magic", one might argue that there still is a sharp difference between a theory that sees emotion as a magical strategy of releasing the agent of a problematic situation, and a theory that sees emotion as a means of apprehending magical qualities found in the world. Given that particular difference among the two theories, regarding the direction of fit between the state and magical qualities, is not Sartre guilty of holding on to two incompatible accounts? The text itself is unfortunately (yet, typically) too condensed to afford a clear answer to that question.

However, there are in my view, some reasons for accepting Sartre's own verdict for the eventual compatibility between the analysis he gives in the final pages of Section III and the main line of argumentation he pursues in the *Sketch* (*STE* 56). The first reason is simple enough: Sartre does not claim to put forward two different theories of a single kind of thing, but to address two different kinds of thing; he explores the phenomenology of two different cases of emotion, but he does not produce two different theories for a single emotion. Thus he writes:

> [T]here are *two forms* of emotion, according to whether it is we who constitute the magic of the world to replace a deterministic activity which cannot be realized, or whether the world itself is unrealizable and reveals itself suddenly as a magical environment. (*STE* 57, emphasis added)

The common feature in both cases of emotion is the presence of magic. Yet, the objection may persist that if the role of magic is so different in the two cases, we do not really have an overarching theory of two kinds of case, but two totally different theories applying themselves to separate cases. Before answering that objection, let me note that it is not identical to the original criticism that Sartre is guilty of pursuing two incompatible lines of reasoning regarding the same phenomenon and that one of those lines is more satisfactory than the other. What we are now seeing is that Sartre is subject at most to the objection that he offers two theories for two different kinds of emotional phenomena, not that he analyses the same phenomenon using two incompatible theories.

Still, the considerations I have presented do not prove that Sartre's approach is internally consistent; what they may offer is some conceptual space for accommodating the "very peculiar phenomena" of horror, terror, wonder and so on within Sartre's theory of emotions. Consider the main example given in the text: "a grimacing face suddenly appears pressed against the outside window; I am frozen with terror" (*STE* 55). Sartre asserts that in this case the emotional apprehension of the corresponding quality (the horrible) is more or less immediate, and is not manifested in fleeing or fainting; we may even think – and Sartre himself does assert – that the particular emotion does not afford talk of "appropriate behaviour" and, thus, that it is an emotion with "no finality" (*STE* 55–6). But, (and here my account diverges from the letter of Sartre's discussion in those pages), we may pose the question that Sartre taught us to raise when it comes to the phenomenology of emotion: why, in the case described, are we frozen with terror? *Prima facie*, it seems that there is no informative way to respond to that question: we just do. Attending to the particulars of the case, though, might give us a more interesting answer. "That face which appears at the window", Sartre astutely observes, "is presented, motionless though it is, as acting at a distance". And how does the subject respond to this fact? He is "frozen with terror". By rendering himself totally inert, "frozen", he might wish that the whole scene, including the threatening presence outside the window, freezes with himself. He aims (magically) to cancel the threat by cancelling its (magical ability of) acting at a distance: what is "frozen" is not only oneself in terror, but also the apparently imminent threat.

It should be noted, of course, that, as we explained during our earlier discussion of the case of fainting out of passive fear for the approaching bear, none of these happen in a cool-headed approach, as calculated steps for the realization of a prudential course of action. Emotion is neither the deliberate employment of means to an end, nor a play that fakes inaction so as to secure particular benefits: in genuine emotion, one's consciousness is not reflective, but out in the world, and lives the significance of the situation with the whole of one's body.[35]

Later on in the narration of his example, Sartre asserts:

> [T]he window and the distance are seized *simultaneously* in the act of consciousness which catches sight of the face at the window: but in the very act of catching sight of it, window and distance are emptied of their necessary character as tools. They are grasped in another way. (*STE* 59)

That way is explicated by Sartre not by proposing some new theory of emotions, but by invoking the main line of reasoning deployed in the *Sketch*, concerning the transformation of the instrumental into the emotional world: "For the horrible *is not possible in the deterministic world of tools*. The horrible can appear only in a world which is such that all the things existing in it are magical by nature, and *the only defences against them are magical*" (*STE* 59, emphasis added).

It is my contention that the discussion of emotion in the final few pages of Section III is in tune with the main account pursued in the *Sketch*. Whether Sartre's numerous remarks about emotion can all be made to fall under a single explanatory heading is an interpretative issue that is admittedly some way from being resolved.

In emotion, consciousness captivates itself by creating a world in which it achieves its objectives through modifications in one's body (including its physiology, posture and activity) that change the way reality is experienced by the subject.[36] But this analysis of emotion in terms of the activity of consciousness raises two fundamental questions about consciousness itself. How can consciousness apprehend the world in more than one way? And what is the structure of conscious activity that enables a subject to experience in some way qualities or entities that, when perceiving the world in a different, non-emotionally, involved way, are not over there? The answer to both questions requires a closer look at the workings of conscious activity. More precisely, it calls for an analysis of Sartre's celebrated theory of imagination; and that will be our topic in the next chapter.

CHAPTER FIVE

Imagining

I

As I look at a horse coming slowly towards me I am presented, in experience, with that elegant animal. Yet seeing something face to face is not the only way for it to appear to us. I may look at a black and white photograph of a horse by the sea, observe Whistler's vivid painting, dream that I am edging ahead at the Grand National, or simply visualize a stallion with its thick hair caressed by the light wind. Looking at pictures, having a dream or just imagining something are all phenomena too ordinary for any theory of human experience to attempt to analyse. A proper analysis of such phenomena, though, encounters a serious puzzle: how is it possible that we are presented with something that is not physically present?

Several philosophers have outlined a story of how to deal with that perplexing aspect of human experience. They usually approach the phenomena as deliverances of a supposedly peculiar faculty whose role is to populate one's consciousness with immaterial entities we call images. Imagination is thus conceived as a failed perception, a weak or defective attempt to launch into reality, that effectively locks oneself inside one's mind. This approach treats perception and imagination on a par, rendering the former a particularly vivid version of the latter, turning the sharp distinction between looking at something, and visualizing it, into a dubious difference of degree.

Sartre sees imagination in a very different light. For him, clarity of philosophical vision brings respect for sharpness of conceptual distinctions. And the concept of "the percept" (what is perceived), is very different from the concept of "the imaginary" (what is imagined). The title of the book we shall examine, *The Imaginary*, is aptly chosen by Sartre for drawing our attention to that which we focus on when we imagine. He thus achieves the strategic goal of making the reader switch into the phenomenological mode of examining the object of consciousness first (how it appears to us, what it is to be an object for consciousness), before we start theorizing about "psychological faculties" or other notions of the traditional metaphysics of mind.

It was not until Sartre's extensive research in the field that a philosophical analysis of imagination was grounded on the phenomena it aims to explain. His treatise on the subject was to become the standard reference for theoretical discussions in this area, and is one of the most influential books of recent times on the nature of imagining.[1] In discussing imagination, Sartre is at his phenomenological best: he brings to light unduly neglected aspects of imagining experience, he dwells on cases that resist a neat categorization, he invokes psychological–experimental evidence that upsets ordinary preconceptions, and he gracefully acknowledges the limits of philosophical discourse on aspects of human experience that seem to escape or, rather, precede conceptualization.

From the wealth of topics addressed in Sartre's treatise, we shall discuss here the fundamental issue of visual imagination. The analysis of visualizing will help us address a series of core theoretical issues concerning the methodology appropriate for a philosophical enquiry into imaginary phenomena, the difference between perceptual and imagining consciousness, the distinction between the content and the object of imagining experience, and, after I support Sartre's dissatisfaction with some standard accounts of the "analogical representative" involved in mental images, I shall offer some critical remarks that tell against the success of Sartre's own account of imagination.

II

Whatever else it might involve, when I imagine my father boarding a train I can easily tell whether what I do is imagining him rather than, say, touching his arm or seeing him in front of me. Yet it is quite puzzling why that is the case. What is it about imagining that makes it so easy to tell that it is an image I now have of my father rather than a perception of him? The puzzle can be resolved if we attend to those features of imagining that constitute its "essence", that is, those characteristics of imagining that mark it as a distinctive type of conscious activity (*IPPI* 4). In the first, and most influential, part of *The Imaginary*, Sartre purports to give us an account of that essence. Before we look at the account, let me raise some methodological issues.

The discussion in the first part is conducted at the level of "The Certain". By that term Sartre intends to capture all those features that make themselves present to consciousness when consciousness turns its attention on its own activity. The problem is that a cursory reading of that part generates the puzzle that some of the features identified by Sartre as evident have been hardly obvious to thinkers who have reflected on such matters. Indeed, a major point made by Sartre is that important thinkers of the past have fallen victims to the "illusion of immanence", according to which in imagining something one is supposedly looking at a picture hanging inside (and thus "immanent to") one's mind (*IPPI* 5, 6, 18, 19, 59). This view might indeed be an illusion, but it is baffling why so many philosophers have endorsed that view if a moment's attention to one's conscious activity presented it as "certain" that imagining has nothing to do with looking at mental pictures.

A response to this problem could appeal to a division of labour: we should distinguish clearly the phenomenological description of conscious experience from the explanation of the phenomena under consideration. Sartre's attack on the illusion of immanence may draw on what is given as "certain" to reflection, but concerns a controversial issue in the philosophical debate over the best explanation of those phenomena. However, that response can be thought to entail that the aim of phenomenological description is simply describing, in no particular order, what is given to consciousness. For Sartre, though, "the first task of [descriptive] psychology is to make [the content of imaginative experience] explicit, describe it, fix it" (*IPPI* 4).[2] Therefore, the overall aim of "The Certain" is not to reiterate what passes through one's mind but to identify the essential features of conscious experience on which a philosophical account of imagination should be based (*IPPI* 5).[3]

A second methodological point concerns the process by which the imaginary material is supplied for phenomenological inspection. Sartre invites us to "produce images in ourselves, reflect on these images, describe them" (*IPPI* 5). The proposal sounds philosophically neutral, but it can be objected that it is a process that privileges a particular type of imaginative experience, wherein images are produced through an act of volition.[4] There is, though, a rather different kind of imagining experience, in which images come unbidden. Those phenomena range from brief spells of daydreaming to the obsessive recurrence of unwelcome images in a subject who is fully awake. Such experiences appear to fall outside the province of deliberate imaginings and, thus, Sartre's method is prejudiced against a significant part of the phenomena of imagination.

The objection is important, but it can be partly met by the following considerations. First, Sartre does examine several cases where the subject feels passive towards the occurrence of mental images, including instances where the subject asserts that she imagines something despite herself, such as in the philosophically hard cases of psychaesthenia, schizophrenia and visual and auditory hallucination. However, that examination takes place in the penultimate part of the book, after the phenomenological description of the standard cases has delivered sufficient material on which to base hypotheses for the adequate interpretation of the relevant phenomena (*IPPI* pt. IV). Second, the Sartrean approach deals with three moments of imaginative experience: the constitution of the image, the appearance of the object thus constituted, and the responses or attitudes taken towards the image. "The Certain" deals with the first two moments of imagining, giving particular emphasis to the second. That preference is, in my view, motivated by Sartre's overall suspicion of the traditional view of mind as creating out of its own stuff an immaterial universe for consciousness to watch. If there is no such mental stuff, and no immaterial qualities that consciousness carries up its sleeve and bestows on its objects, then it is not in the so-called mental faculties that one should look for the characteristics of the imagined object, but in the way the object itself appears to consciousness when it is imagined. Therefore, Sartre may feel justified in commencing his phenomenological analysis by focusing on that aspect of imagination – namely, the object imagined – whose description can proceed independently of traditional philosophical doctrines, and whose understanding is a precondition for an adequate interpretation of imagining experience, whatever form that experience might take, unbidden, compulsive or deliberate.

Nevertheless, there is a remaining worry that is hardly addressed by Sartre or his commentators.[5] The Sartrean approach bets on the hypothesis that, in its essential features, how an imagined object appears to consciousness is independent of whether its imagining was willed or unbidden. Sartre, I think, wins on his bet. However, that does not justify the assumption that the activity of producing images by an act of volition leaves unaffected the phenomenology of what is thus imagined. And that is precisely the methodological point I have raised.

Finally, there is a methodological problem regarding the very possibility of attending to imagining experience. Under normal circumstances, in imagining something one is simply absorbed in what one imagines. Trying to keep one's reflective gaze fixed on consciousness as it is imagining something might thus produce theoretical cross-eyedness. Sartre notes this problem in his discussion of the elusiveness of imagination (*IPPI* ch. 2). We may attempt to overcome this problem by exploiting the resources of instant memory, producing an image of, say, a chair, and then constructing from memory how the chair as imaged appeared to consciousness in the moment that has passed. It might be thought that the non-coincidence of the memory with what is remembered creates sufficient distance for consciousness to fix on its imagining activities without itself being involved in the activity that has already passed. The difficulty with this proposal is that, within the phenomenological tradition at least, the memory of something involves not the observation of immaterial copies of past objects or events, but the reviving of the conscious activity that intended those objects or events.[6] However, if that reviving includes the actual replay of the original imaginative act, then the initial problem of double theoretical vision would be reiterated (only further complicated by the introduction of the third item: that of remembering the conscious act on which reflection is directed).

It seems to me that Sartre surmounts this problem via a different route, that is, by bringing to the open the awareness consciousness has of itself while it is imagining something. As we have noted several times already, consciousness is non-positionally aware of itself being positionally conscious (in thought, perception or imagination) of its intentional object. Sartre's standard procedure in the first part of his book is to make explicit the awareness implicit in the very act of imagining.[7] As far as the analysis of imaginary phenomena is concerned, it is an approach that seems to deal effectively with a problem that is not exclusive to Sartre's project, but affects any attempt to build a theory of imagination on the evidence supplied by the agent's own experience. A non-negligible virtue of Sartre's approach is its methodological modesty. Having spent around ten pages identifying and lucidly describing some essential characteristics of the experience of imagining, Sartre asserts that it would be wrong to proceed further without recourse to broader philosophical considerations, comparative enquiries and empirical (behavioural, psychological, linguistic and physiological) data: "Simple reflection, it seems to us, has delivered all that it can" (*IPPI* 15).[8]

What reflection delivered in Sartre's case is the material for one of the most insightful analyses of imagining. Sartre's text resists a simple review and the interested reader is strongly advised to look at the text itself for a subtle and illuminating narrative of imaginative experience. What I propose to offer instead is a systematization of his various remarks on how imagining consciousness relates to its objects. To that end, I shall focus on the distinguishing features of the intentional act and its object when something is imagined, and perceived, so as to gain a better understanding of the Sartrean approach to "the two great irreducible attitudes of consciousness" (*IPPI* 120).

III

Look at the open book in front of you. Then close your eyes, and imagine it. What was it that you just imagined? Well, obviously, you imagined the book that lies in front of you. The object at which your imagining is directed is the book that you now have started reading again. This all might sound trivial but it is of great philosophical import. That way of recounting your experience implies that what you imagined was (not a picture, or a copy, or a photo, or an image of a book, but) the book: to imagine something is not to see an image of it (*IPPI* 52). Imagining does not involve three entities: yourself, an image and an object. Rather, it is a distinctive way or "attitude" through which consciousness intends a particular object: to have an image of something is neither more nor less than to have an imaginative consciousness of that thing. An image, in other words, is not the positional object of consciousness but a way in which consciousness intends its object.[9]

We could extend this line of reasoning to the point of denying that there are such things as mental images. Sartre could be thus interpreted as an eliminativist, anticipating a number of recent philosophers who consider talk of mental images as devoid of reference.[10] That eliminativist reading, though, is resisted by Sartre's text. In considering the option of denying "the existence of mental images", Sartre asserts that such a "radical solution is contradicted by the data of introspection", since we can "at will, imagine a horse, a tree, a house" (*IPPI* 6).[11] It seems to me that what Sartre is really opposed to here is the doctrine that denies the reality of the experience of images.[12] He would thus decline the characterization of "eliminativist" if it committed him to the view that consciousness was somehow systematically misled into believing that it forms images of objects. However, his wholesale attack on the "classical theories" of imagination makes the retention of the term "mental image" problematic; it might be acceptable to hold on to that term only if it is employed as shorthand for the phrase "imaging consciousness of an object".[13]

As far as the reality of "the experience of images" is concerned, it would be good to ascertain whether it refers to the alleged experience of looking at an immaterial entity commonly referred to as a "mental image", or whether it denotes the phenomenon of experiencing something as of an image, whereby one is implicitly aware of attending to something as imaged – in contrast, for instance, to being perceived. Sartre would deny the former option, since he denies that there are such peculiar entities for us to have an experience of them. The latter phenomenon should therefore be the focus of our analysis. Let us proceed by considering more closely our example of imaging a particular book.

With your eyes closed, consciousness intended the book as its intentional target, and that intending was experienced as, in crucial respects, different from perceiving that same item. But in what exactly does that difference consist? It cannot simply be a matter of whether your eyes were open or not: although having your eyes open is necessary for vision, it is not *per se* excluding the activity of imagination. First of all, imagining can be, and most of the time is, actually done with one's eyes open. Second, the movement of our eyes might be relevant to certain forms of visualizing, but has no part in sensory imagination that operates in a non-visual mode, such as imagining the beginning of a melody, dialogue in your radio play, the roughness of sandpaper, or the smell of beef stew.[14] There is, finally, a vast domain of imaginative experience in which we form, test or elaborate hypotheses without involving any sensory modality. We may subsume this type of experience under the category of "imagining-that" something is the case: sometimes also referred to as "propositional imagining", in contrast to "perceptual imagining".[15] However, I shall not dwell here on this type of imagination, for two reasons. First, Sartre focuses on forms of imagining consciousness that match our perceptual modalities (especially sight and hearing), and for which he employs the term "imaging", so as to highlight that it is the presentation of objects under their sensible aspects he is interested in;[16] second, even when he discusses cases of imagining a situation or a series of events extended through time, Sartre's analysis is cast in terms of the imaging activities of visualizing and audializing (*IPPI* IV, III).

IV

A better way to approach the difference between imaging and perceiving is to reflect on how the object appears when perceived and when imaged.

An imaged object shows itself orientated in a certain way, in virtue of which only a particular aspect of the object appears to us. The object thus seems to have a "sensible opacity", yet it appears to lack any real depth (*IPPI* 10). That impression is reinforced by the peculiarly tight relation that holds between the imagined object and space: as the object moves so does its space. In fact, the space of the imaged object is rather like a halo that surrounds the object in its imaginary adventures. The exact limits of that halo are hard to determine; its margins are essentially vague, neither fixed by the contours of the object, nor extending far beyond it. In contrast to perceived objects that occupy and move in and through space, imaged objects seem not to traverse any distance so much as to carry their own space with them. No wonder relations among imaged objects seem impossible to determine; to measure any two items they must occupy a common space, but shared space is a feature of perceived, not imaged, objects. Note that the same indeterminacy applies in cases where one images a scene with two or more objects. The exact distance between a horse, say, and a palm tree is not something that can be revealed to the subject, however hard one "observes" the imaged scene. And if you decide that the imaged distance is, for instance, four metres, there is still no criterion of correctness for your judgement except your decreeing that for a distance to be four metres, it must be how far the one object appears to you to be from the other.

That lack of fixed measures is indicative of the overall lack of determinations characterizing imaged objects. There are no set distances between any two points of an imaged object. Even in cases where one imagines an object along given specifications (e.g. by following the instruction of forming the image of a terracotta vase whose right handle is twelve centimetres from its left) one is not able to check that the object imaged fits the specifications, for example by bringing forwards the imaged vase, so as to apply your mental tape measure to it. The distance or any other relation among features of an object is not something that you discover but something that you, in the very act of imagining, make so: the imaged vase cannot check your judgement, since what and how a thing is imagined co-varies with your imagining it.

An important implication of the above considerations is that, contrary to popular – and philosophical – preconceptions, the world of imagination might not be as exciting as one might initially think. In comparing the world of perception with that of imagination, Sartre's preferences for the former are hard to mistake (*IPPI* 8–11, 128–30). A perceived object always has more to give you than a quick glance reveals to you. The longer you observe it, the more details about itself will become evident to you: its surroundings; its relations, matches and contrasts with other objects. In turning an object around, or in making a tour of it, new aspects will come into view, and the previous aspects will acquire all sorts of practical, aesthetic or other dimensions that might not have been obvious before. An object encountered is, as Sartre puts it, overflowing our experience; neither our perceptual takes on it nor our descriptive accounts can exhaust all that is ever possible to experience of, or to say about, that thing (*IPPI* 10).

The imaged object, by contrast, is characterized by an "essential poverty" (*IPPI* 9). It is not only a lack of detail in the colour, texture, shape or outline of the imaged object that accounts for its poverty in sensible content. It is also the striking absence of relations with other objects or features of the world. Every perceptible object is in a large, if not infinite, number of relations with other objects in its environment; indeed, a wealth of relations to other objects goes hand in hand with the object's individuality. It is precisely because an object is exactly what it is and not another thing that it finds itself in innumerable relations with other things constituting the world of sense experience. An imaged object, on the other hand, enjoys a very limited set of relations both internally and externally: "The different elements of an image maintain no relations with the rest of the world and maintain only two or three relations between themselves: those, for example, that I could note, or those that is presently important to retain" (*IPPI* 9). The paucity of internal and external relations and the lack of various kinds of determination combine in the arising of the feeling that attending to an imaged object makes at best for "quasi-observation". Observing an imaged object does not promise any revelation, since however hard I attend to it, "I will never find anything there but what I put there" (*IPPI* 9).[17]

The last remark, although obvious, should be treated with some care. To me it does not sound like a phenomenological claim, but an explanatory note on the nature of imagining experience. It might therefore be worth specifying the phenomenological grounds for Sartre's claim that imaged objects appear as they do because we somehow make them to appear thus and so.

One reason that can be offered in support of this claim is that we experience no time lag between the imaged object and the imaging consciousness (*IPPI* 11). The problem, though, is that this fact can be subject to different interpretations. The simultaneity of imaging consciousness and imaged object means that the latter does not precede the former; hence the object does not exist as imaged in advance of our imagining it in one way or another. However, it can be argued that for an object to owe its constitution – or, at least, its manner of appearing – to some other thing, that other thing should precede the object that it determines. But the simultaneity of consciousness and object appears to preclude the scenario of the object being what it is because the imagining consciousness occurs first, and a moment or two later the object, as an independent product, makes its appearance. Furthermore, that claim would be falsified by ordinary experience, and Sartre certainly admits as much.

The problem, perhaps, is generated by the assumption that we have so far been concerned with the temporal relation between two "things". But consciousness is not a thing, it is an intentional "aiming at", a "directedness toward" things. In imagining a vase, our previously acquired knowledge (about vases) and a current intention (to form an image of a specimen) are "indissolubly linked" in the synthetic act of imagining the object. Neither the imagined object nor the consciousness intending it can exist separately, since for an object to appear as imaged is just consciousness intending that object in the image form: "the intention reveals itself at the same time as it realizes itself, in and by its realization" (*IPPI* 11).

The indissoluble link between knowledge and intention may further illuminate why the Sartrean realist is not in a hurry to leave the world of perception for the universe of imagination. The fact that no imaging intention can be formed without some knowledge about what is imaged and about how the thing imaged looks (sounds, feels), entails that in imagining there is "not a second of surprise" (*IPPI* 11). To be sure, one's imaginings can be accompanied by a feeling of surprise about oneself: more precisely, about one's ability to follow through the instructions in imaging a cube, changing its colour and rotating it 180 degrees, or about one's ability to give a really adequate description of what an imaged object looks like. But the surprise does not come from the part of the imaged object itself. We do not often hear someone say, "I was really surprised that the brown horse that I imagined turned out to be white". To imagine something with different colours is not a process of getting to know more about a fixed thing, but of imagining different things.

V

We have so far focused on the differences between the appearance of an object in imagination and its appearance in perception. The way something looks – regarding its shape, volume, depth, relation to other things, the location in and movement through space – is sharply different when it is perceived and when it is imagined. Those differences seem to remove in large part the mystery that initially surrounded the question of why it seems so simple to tell whether I now imagine – rather than perceive – a horse galloping by the sea: a horse imaged just looks so differently from a horse perceived.

It is not only the objects, though, of the acts of imagination and perception that appear very different, it is also those acts themselves. Their difference consists in the way each of those acts posits – sets before itself – its object. The positing of perceptual consciousness involves the affirmation of the object's current existence in the subject's perceptual field. Perception, in other words, comes with a belief in the presence of its intended object. Imagination, on the other hand, denies existence of its objects in four possible ways: by directly positing the object as non-existent, by positing it as not currently present or as existing elsewhere, or by withholding any commitment as to its existence (*IPPI* 12).

The lack of existence is not an extra feature "superimposed" on the image after it is formed. The positing of an object as absent or non-existent "is constitutive of the image consciousness" (*IPPI* 13). To think otherwise would lead us to the twin errors of idealist metaphysics and false phenomenology. Sartre is rather brief on this issue, so let me spell out what I think is his underlying reasoning on this point.

The "superimposition" thesis would imply that there is an object fully formed inside one's mind for us to watch and that two of our mental faculties – perception and imagination – vie to possess it: if existence is added to that internal object, the object passes to perception; if existence is denied it, the object goes to imagination. A first problem with that account is that it underestimates the radical difference in nature between the imaginary and the perceived. As we saw in the previous section, how something appears to consciousness when it is imaged is very different from how it appears when it is perceived. Therefore, the claim that there is a fixed object that appears in an identical manner to both perception and imagination is falsified by the facts of ordinary conscious experience.

A second problem with the superimposition thesis is the lack of phenomenological evidence in its support. We just do not seem to first imagine something and then subtract presence from it. I do not, for instance, form the image of Pierre having a stroll in East Berlin, and then consider whether or not what I intend is actually in front of me. Hence, in imagination, consciousness does not "reduce" the reality of the scene after it has intended that scene: to imagine a scene is already to intend it as not presently occurring. Sartre illustrates this point with an apposite remark:

> If the image of a dead loved one appears to me abruptly, there is no need for a "reduction" to feel the ache in my heart: it is

> part of the image, it is the direct consequence of the fact that the image gives its object as a nothingness of being. (*IPPI* 13)

The third and, in a sense, the most fundamental problem with the superimposition thesis is that it is premised on the assumption that what is aimed at by consciousness is an internal immaterial object that is made available to either perception or imagination. Sartre, though, believes that no such internal object exists: in imagination, no less than in perception, whatever consciousness is directed at is outside consciousness (*IPPI* 53). When I imagine Pierre walking by the Brandenburg Gate, neither that stone edifice nor my friend are inside my consciousness: whatever that "inside" is taken to mean. If it is taken in the physical sense, the material entities (Pierre and the Brandenburg Gate) cannot possibly be inside my consciousness, which is not even a three-dimensional thing. If it is taken in the intentional sense, the entities imaged (Pierre and the Brandenburg Gate) are not immanent to consciousness but, as Sartre puts, it, transcendent to it: they are those objects towards which consciousness is directed. Either way, the claim that what is imaged is an "internal" object seriously misrepresents the intentional structure of conscious activity.

VI

The phenomenological source of the puzzle of imagination is that the object as perceived looks different from how it looks as imaged. The traditional response to the puzzle is that the difference in "looks" is really a difference in objects; in conscious activity we deal with two different kinds of object, one being the object imaged, the other the object encountered in perception. Sartre, on the contrary, states that it is one and the same object intended in two different ways. The world does not contain things imagined located next to, beneath or above things perceived. There is only one reality intended in two different ways.

Imagining is a way in which consciousness intends its object. The notion of "object", though, is itself in need of some clarification. Consider first the kinds of thing we imagine: they can be an entity (a vase), an event (the vase falling on the floor) or a state of affairs (that the vase is no longer on the shelf). When Sartre enquires about the object of the imaging act, he is focusing on single entities (a chair, the hidden arabesques of a wall tapestry, or Pierre; see e.g. *IPPI* 3, 7, 12, 119, 120). He is interested, in other words, in entities as imaged. We may refer to such entities in response to the question "What is it that you image?" An answer to that question, though, might refer ambiguously to both the object and the content of a mental act. And this raises a crucial issue in philosophy of mind. Which of those two things, the content or the object, is "before our mind" in an imaging act?

According to one line of reasoning, imaging consciousness cannot be intentionally related to an object. A relation relates things that exist. The alleged object of imagination is non-existent. Hence, there cannot be an intentional relation between imaging and an object. Imaging, however, is not devoid of content: we can always give some answer to the question "What is it that you image?"; we cannot image without imaging something, whatever that might be. Therefore, imaging is an intentional relation, not to an object, but to a content.

This line of reasoning is bold, and comes with a strong philosophical pedigree.[18] Its conclusion, though, is problematic. The source of the problem is its view of intentional content. That view makes content dependent on an intentional object. A mental act intends its object always in a particular way; the object appears from a particular angle, or at a certain distance, showing itself under this or that particular aspect. Call this the "aspectual shape" of the object. To talk about the "content" of the mental act is then understood as talking about "the intentional object with its aspectual shape" (Searle 1992: 155; cf. Crane 2001: 38). However, if content is defined in terms of object, it is not clear to me how there can be intentional acts that lack the latter but retain the former.

We can express the same worry in the form of a dilemma. Imaging is either contentful or it is not. If it is not, then it cannot consist in a relation to an intentional content. But if it is, it cannot involve a relation to a content without intending the object in virtue of which such content exists in the first place. The dilemma shows that we cannot bypass the issue of the intentional object by postulating content as the focus of imaging intention.

The intentional object holds a prominent place in the Sartrean analysis of imaging consciousness. The opening and closing remarks of *The*

Imaginary are devoted to a clarification of what exactly the intentional object of an imaging act is. However, the Sartrean approach appears to suffer from the opposite problem to that which affected the previous theory. Whereas that theory of imaging banished the intentional object from its account, the Sartrean emphasis on object seems to work against the reality of content. The paucity of references to "mental content", and the absence of a section dedicated to that notion, might give the impression that the concept of mental content has been excluded from the Sartrean system. The impression is reinforced if we recall the attack on content launched in Sartre's early paper "Intentionality". A commitment to mental content was there taken as the trademark of "digestive" philosophies, with their idealist predilection for an all-consuming mind, which swallows material things, turns them into immaterial entities, stores them in a spiritual container, and constructs out of them a simulacrum of reality.

Sartre's early attack on digestive philosophy was gradually developed into a detailed critique of philosophical doctrines – common to both idealist and empiricist schools of thought – that give a distorted picture of human experience (see esp. *Ion* chs 1–2). However, as his critique of the traditional view of mind became subtler, so his attack on mental content became qualified. By the time of the publication of his second work on imagination, the notion of mental content seems fully rehabilitated.[19] I would maintain that if *The Imaginary* includes no section headed "mental content", that is not because content is kept in exile, but because it is a notion underlying much of the discussion in each chapter, making it necessary to employ a variety of terms that would specify which particular aspect of content is under consideration in the course of each discussion. Thus Sartre talks about "matter", "*hyle*", "analogon" and "psychic datum" (see e.g. *IPPI* 50, 51, 53). The most interesting among those notions, and the one that has attracted most philosophical attention, is the notion of the "analogon". Let me explicate this notion, and to explain why its use generates problems that Sartre's theory appears unable to resolve.

VII

Consider the case of seeing a portrait. A painting hangs on a gallery wall, and by looking at it, you see the face of, say, Jacqueline Du Pré. The painted canvas counts as a portrait because you see a face in it. The material thing in front of you is so marked, coloured and, in a word, "manipulated" that the face of someone absent is presented to you. Your consciousness intends that person by responding to the painting in a particular way. Hence, there are at least three elements involved in the seeing of something in a painting: an intention that aims at that thing; a matter that the intention transforms; and the thing aimed at that is not present.

To be sure, seeing, in this case, does not come on its own. There is background knowledge (acquired perhaps by seeing in the past the face of the famous cellist on CD covers), knowledge that helps you identify what you see in the painting as the face of that particular person; and there is an affective response to features accentuated or otherwise emphasized in the painting, which make you feel in the presence of the uniquely gifted yet tragic figure of recent music history.

The painting supplies the material that our visual intention animates so as to let something that is not actually in front us become present.[20] The painted canvas is not experienced as an indifferent object but as a portrait, that is, as something that solicits our seeing in it the face of the absent person. In the normal run of things, the reception of something as a portrait is the intended result of the act of drawing, marking, colouring or, in general, creating a marked surface whose visible aspects, especially its outline, shape and composition, resemble the person pictured (*IPPI* 24).[21] The resemblance of the portrait to the person portrayed is one way in which something perceived functions as the analogical representative of the pictured object. "Analogon" is the term Sartre coins for denoting any type of content, awareness of which presents us with an absent object.

Putting the above points together gives us a definition of image as "an act that aims in its corporeality at an absent or non-existent object, through a physical or psychic content that is given not as itself but in the capacity of 'analogical representative' of the object aimed at" (*IPPI* 20). When the content is "physical", the image may include the perception of a photo, a film screen, a painting, a sketch, a line drawing or anything else (such as a mime performance) that solicits the appearance of some absent person, object or scene. If the content, though, that our intention animates is "psychic" then there occurs a "mental" image.

To assess the justifiability of this scheme, it would help to consider three questions. Why talk about an "analogon" at all in the case of mental images? What is the analogon of a mental image according to standard accounts of imagination? What is put forward as the analogon of a mental image by Sartre himself? I shall answer those questions in a way that highlights the difficulties Sartre invites by subscribing to the idea of the "analogon".

VIII

The analogon is not something revealed by phenomenological analysis. When I imagine Pierre, there is no in-between matter, no psychic canvas that I animate with a view to reaching an absent object: the imaged Pierre is directly presented to me as absent. Sartre does not deny that the experience of imaging someone is that of being directly intending that person, without first having to watch a psychic intermediary of mental stuff (the way one has to see the physical intermediary of the painted canvas if one is to see something in it). Yet he seems to hold on to the existence of a psychic intermediary endowed with a somehow lesser existence than their physical equivalents, material pictures. He admits, for instance, that, contrary to the painted surface of a canvas, which can be perceived in a number of different ways (visually, observing its patches of colour; tactilely, running the tip of our fingers through its corners; even olfactorily, checking, for example, for the presence of varnish or other preservatives), and which can, as an object, exist well before and after our visit to the art gallery, "the matter [of a mental image] has so little independence that it appears with the image and disappears with it" (*IPPI* 24). But "little independence" is already too much: in imaging Pierre, consciousness seems aware of no thing awaiting observation so as to get to Pierre by way of seeing that thing; nor is there any matter of the image left after consciousness ceased imaging, available for consciousness to examine in its own right: "when consciousness is annihilated, its ... content is annihilated with it ... there remains no residue that can be described" (*IPPI* 53).

Note that the perfect simultaneity between imaging an object and the existence of the analogon of the object imaged may not on its own tell against the reality of the analogon. After all, we could perhaps conceive of a universe where portraits sprang into existence the very moment one turned one's gaze at them, and ceased to exist as soon as one stopped looking at them. Even in that universe we could in principle observe and examine the physical analogon on its own, for its various sensible and compositional properties *vis-à-vis* its role as a material representative of the pictured object. However, such an independent examination of the analogon is not available in the case of mental images. The simultaneous existence of imaging and of the psychic analogon is a source of philosophical worry because it indicates that we have no independent hold on the notion of the analogon, except for its postulation as a psychic stand-in of the imaged object.

IX

Recall that, according to Sartre's own phenomenological enquiry, to form an image of Pierre is not to imagine an image (be it mental or physical) of Pierre. Imagining is an act directed not at images, but at objects themselves when absent from the agent's perceptual field; an image is "a certain way that an object has of being absent within its very presence" (*IPPI* 85).

The puzzlement that is understandably generated by this phenomenon has led theorists of the past to think of images as substitute entities. On that account, what consciousness is directed at is a thing in miniature, which inhabits the mind, and which carries the exact qualities of the thing it represents. The psychic miniature represents the real thing precisely because it shares with it those qualities that lead imaging consciousness from the immanent copy to the transcendent original. Alas, by transferring to the psychic content the qualities of the imaged object, philosophers of the past fall prey to the illusion of immanence, or so Sartre contends (*IPPI* 87–8). Before we discuss the Sartrean way out of this problem, let me explain why, in my view, Sartre is right to attack past theories of this matter as philosophically implausible.

There are two kinds of reason why the miniature story is unlikely to be true. On the one hand, it is hard to think what might fill the role of such a miniature. If it is to be a tiny material object, whose ability to represent something is due to its sharing with the original thing various sensible properties (shape, colour, etc.), then that material miniature does not match our ordinary conception of a mental image. To use a simple example, an image of a ripe yellow banana does not appear itself to be curved, yellow and ready to eat. We cannot literally change the colour of that image (e.g. by applying red dye to it), and even if we switch from the image of a yellow banana to that of a red banana, that is not because we have in any way altered the colour of the yellow banana, but because we have now started imagining something different. If, though, the miniature entity is to be immaterial, then it becomes even harder to understand how a non-material object can bear sensible properties such as shape, colour and so on.[22]

The other kind of reason for not accepting a miniature entity as the analogon that stands in for the imaged object is that the structure of imagining is not the one of seeing one object by looking at something else. That is by now our familiar fact that the phenomenology of mental imaging does not exemplify the indirect structure of perceiving a portrait. In imagining, we are directly presented with Pierre as imaged, and not with some other thing (a miniature, a canvas, a piece of printed paper) in which, or through which, we can make out Pierre.

Can Sartre improve on the standard accounts of the "matter" of mental images? We may answer this question by considering his suggested candidate for the role of the analogon.

X

In his discussion of the analogon, extended through seven chapters of *The Imaginary*, Sartre identifies three elements that come together to form the imaging attitude: "knowledge", "affectivity" and "kinaesthetic sensations". Let us briefly examine each one in turn.

"Knowledge" refers to the cognitive content that informs our intention of imaging someone or something as a particular entity or, at least, as an instance of a particular kind of entity. I can, for instance, respond successfully to the instruction "form the image of a cube" because I possess knowledge about the shape of that geometrical object. Similarly, I can recognize an image that came to my mind unbidden as an image of the Eiffel Tower, seen from the exit of Trocadéro Métro station, because I have relevant background knowledge that goes into the formation of that image.

Knowledge, however, does not come on its own; it brings with it – we might even say, in it – a felt quality that corresponds to the affective properties of the object or of the scene imaged. To stay with our Paris example: imaging a metal edifice from that particular viewpoint is, for me, to intend the Eiffel Tower, because to that viewpoint there are attached feelings (e.g. of longing, of travel fatigue, of the peculiar numbness following a cancelled rendezvous), which give an affective texture to the experience. It is therefore the imaging not of any old metal construction, but of the Eiffel Tower, as seen by someone rushing out of Trocadéro Métro station.

What about the third element of the Sartrean account, the "kinaesthetic sensations"? To get a taste of how this notion works in Sartre's system, try to image the Eiffel Tower – taking in, in your imagination, the whole of it from bottom to top – without moving your retinas upwards and downwards; or try to image a moving pendulum without letting your eyes swing from right to left, back and fro. Sartre bets that it cannot be done, and he offers this fact as presenting an instance of the general rule that in imaging something our conscious intention animates sensations of our body, dressing them, one might say, with the shapes of the image world (*IPPI* 78–83).[23]

If that approach to imagination could be adequately developed, its advantages over the traditional competitors would be considerable. It does not present the analogon as a miniature object watched by consciousness, and thus avoids the above-mentioned difficulties involved in explicating what type of object (material or immaterial) could supposedly intervene between consciousness and the imaged object. Indeed, the Sartrean approach appears to do away with the indirect structure of seeing one object in another (taken over from the case of seeing something in a physical picture), and to preserve the autonomy of imagination as one of "the irreducible attitudes of consciousness" (*IPPI* 120).

I believe, though, that Sartre's approach faces problems of its own. The first is what we might call the problem of discrimination. The retinal movement (or, for that matter, any other bodily movement whose awareness is supposedly involved) in imaging the Eiffel Tower, from the ground to the top, might not be very different from the retinal movement in imaging the Empire State Building from its ground entrance to its spire at the top. The same problem applies to the cases of imaging a garden swing and a steel pendulum, or indeed, any two or more objects whose pattern of movement, or outline shape, is more or less identical. Yet, we have no difficulty telling that what we imagine is a swing hanging from two trees or a small pendulum decorating an office desk. Therefore, invoking the Sartrean analogon of kinaesthetic sensations cannot help explain the obvious differences in the things imaged, when those things are represented (in their outline shape or pattern of movement) by the same kinaesthetic sensations.

The second problem is what might be referred to as the problem of comprehensiveness. Awareness of bodily movement (be it of the retina, of our index finger, or of any other moving part; *IPPI* 74–8, 80–81, 134) is not a sufficient ground for all the sensible properties of things imaged. Imagine a transparent cube, and then imagine a cube of the same size but of red colour, or of yellow, or of purple. The colour of the thing imaged will in each case be different; yet the outline shape, which is (supposedly) grounded on the feeling of retinal movement, is clearly the same. Therefore, the Sartrean hypothesis of the kineasthetic analogon leaves out properties – such as colours – that are an indispensable part of many an imagining experience.

It might be worth clarifying the nature of the critical remarks I made against the Sartrean view of the analogon. It was granted that Sartre discusses the analogon as part of an explanatory story of the phenomena of imagination. References to the analogon do not form part of his phenomenological description of how consciousness intends the imaged object; on the contrary, Sartre is keen to underline that the analogon of a mental image, even though it is not appearing to unreflective consciousness, is something that should exist, given the structure of imaging experience in general (whether, for instance, we intend a painting, a printed image or a mental image). Hence, one might respond to my critical remarks by stating that they target the phenomenological shortcomings of the Sartrean theory of the analogon, whereas that theory presents an explanatory hypothesis, not a phenomenological account of imaginary experience.

However, that is not how my criticism works. The worries I expressed concern the ability of the Sartrean theory to explain the phenomena under consideration. As an explanatory hypothesis, the idea of the kinaesthetic analogon is shown inadequate to the twin tasks of (i) telling apart experiences of imaged objects that are clearly different, and (ii) covering an essential aspect of any visualization that intends its object in its various sensible (including its colour) qualities. I have not brought into the discussion considerations external to Sartre's way of thinking about imagination,[24] nor have I sought to stress implicit inconsistencies between some of his phenomenological statements.[25] My point has been that, even if we take Sartre at his own words, the philosophical task of giving a satisfactory analysis of the "analogon" of mental image remains ahead of us.

XI

We began this chapter by posing the rather common question of how it is possible for us, in imagination, to somehow be presented with things not physically present. The philosophical sense of that question concerns the conditions of the possibility of imagination. It aims, in other words, to an explication of what should be the case for consciousness to be able to intend things as being otherwise than they really are.

If the above question sounds philosophically pressing, if, in uttering it, we seem to express a serious puzzlement as to the very possibility of the phenomena of imagining, that might be due to an underlying assumption about what consciousness is, and how it supposedly works. We seem, to put it differently, to come to the question of the alleged "peculiarity" of imagination, having already decided (if we ever thought about it) how consciousness works in the "normal" run of things. It might, I think, be more fruitful and, from a phenomenological standpoint, less prejudicial, to reverse the order of explication by asking what consciousness is, given its ability to imagine. That ability is not a mere, or a rare disposition: it is something ordinarily and effortlessly realized, in our daily transaction with the physical and social world.

Accordingly, in the final chapter of his treatise, Sartre asks: "what are the characteristics that can be attributed to consciousness on the basis of the fact that it is consciousness capable of imagining?" (*IPPI* 179). That question is soon substituted by a different one: "is the function of imagining a contingent ... specification of the essence 'consciousness' or should it rather be described as a constitutive structure of this essence?" (*IPPI* 179). The former question invites the derivation of other characteristics of consciousness on the basis of its ability to imagine; the latter question stays with that ability, and probes the ability's relation to the essence of consciousness. Recall that, according to Sartre, consciousness is necessarily consciousness of something, or, as he puts it in that chapter: "it is in the very nature of consciousness to be intentional and a consciousness that ceased to be consciousness of something would thereby cease to exist" (*IPPI* 183). Intentionality, being the essential characteristic of conscious experience, will set up a train of reasoning that will arrive at the conclusion that "imagination, far from appearing as an accidental characteristic of consciousness, is disclosed as an essential and transcendental condition of consciousness" (*IPPI* 188). My aim in this section is to reconstruct that piece of Sartre's reasoning. Here is how, I think, it goes.

To imagine is to posit an object as "irreal". We can posit something as irreal only on the background of what is experienced as real. The imaged object is something that consciousness constitutes through isolating that thing from its actual environment, and annihilating it, that is, intending that object as not being part of or in the world. Negating the worldly status of an object, however, is only possible if one has a sense of there being a world. In perception, objects are posited as real because they are presented against the background of the synthetic totality of spatiotemporal, physical, practical and other relations that constitute the world. Having a sense of the world, though, presupposes the ability to stand back, and take in what is occurring in one's experience as being an event in the world, to intend what is encountered as being located in the world, to engage in practical activities as unfolding in the world and so on. The constitution of the world implies the ability of consciousness to stand back and intend the world as the meaningful synthesis of the items that make up reality. This "standing back" of consciousness, its ability to withdraw from the given, so that it may then be able to intend it in its multiple significations, is nothing other than the ability required to set something before oneself as irreal.

"We must bear in mind", Sartre writes, "that the act of positing the world as a synthetic totality and the act of 'standing back' from the world are one the same act" (*IPPI* 184). The puzzle of imagination was generated by the worry about how it is possible for consciousness to withdraw from the real and to constitute objects as irreal. The key to the puzzle is that without the ability of consciousness to stand back, and intend things as being an integral part of a network of objects and events that far exceeds the individual item on which consciousness is focused, we would have no sense of reality, no awareness of there being a world. It is because consciousness is not exhausted in the individual item (side, aspect or part of a thing) currently perceived, that it can intend the whole object – any perceptible object – as real. But that is also what is required for the activity of imagination, that is, for intending objects in a way different from the exact way they are given to us. It is because consciousness is not overdetermined by what is immediately given to it that it can intend whole objects as being what they are (in perceiving) and as being different from what they are (in imagining). The ability to transcend the given is the fundamental precondition for both perception and imagination; and – to complete that section of the Sartrean reasoning – since we think there is nothing extraordinary in realizing that ability in the case of perception, we should think the same in the case of imagination.

That is a truly interesting argument, but it is not clear that it serves the goal set by Sartre himself. What Sartre was setting out to establish was that imagination is nothing less than a "constitutive structure of the essence" of consciousness. Instead, what he appears to have shown, so far, is that a major activity of consciousness – that of being directed at perceptible objects – requires the very same ability activated in the case of intending objects as imaged. More simply expressed, my point is that what the Sartrean argument has delivered (if successful) is that an essential ability of consciousness is employed also in imagining things, not that imagining things is an essential ability of consciousness. Can we move from the former claim to the latter?

The move is, I think, effected in a complex manner, as it reaches completion in several steps. The first step capitalizes on the ability of consciousness to stand back from the instantaneous given so as to synthesize things into a meaningful whole. Sartre gives this ability a name no less potent than that of "freedom": "to posit reality as a synthetic whole is enough to posit oneself as free from it and this surpassing is freedom itself since it could not be effected were consciousness not free" (*IPPI* 184). It is worth noting how straightforward and specific the introduction of "freedom itself" is in the Sartrean system; popular misconceptions to the contrary, there are no political, moral, humanistic, theistic or secular overtones in Sartre's primary use of the notion of freedom. Instead, it is a notion employed to convey something revealed by the analysis of conscious activity.

The "surpassing" mentioned in the above quote is the next important concept for our argument. Surpassing never happens in a void. It involves, instead, three specific dimensions: there is something that gets surpassed, from a certain point of view, towards something that was not given to consciousness in advance of that activity. In the simplest case, the facing side of a cube is surpassed from my spatiotemporal standpoint towards the totality of its sides, so that perceptual awareness of a whole object is duly formed. However, surpassing is not limited to the perceptual case, and its function is not exclusively representational. In a side remark, that, in my view, is crucial for bringing imagination to the heart of this argument, Sartre notes that "there are in fact, for consciousness, many other ways to surpass the real in order to make a world of it: the surpassing can and should be made made first by affectivity or by action" (*IPPI* 185). To appreciate the significance of that remark, think of what is involved in attending to the world as an agent: someone acts in the light of how things are (perceived by him to be), from a particular (spatiotemporal, practical, emotional or other) standpoint, towards realizing his view of how things ought to be.[26] Being able to intend things as being otherwise than they are is a necessary condition for acting so as to effect changes that would make the real world fit one's "irreal view" of it. Within that view, I "negate" certain aspects of a real object (some of its current qualities, or dimensions, or location, or relations to other things) and intend that object, under its sensible aspect, in different ways (having different qualities, dimensions, location or factual relations) than the ones perceived. But what is that ability but imagination itself?

Three qualifications of the above account are in order. First, our reconstruction sharpens the distinction between different conscious activities that are not, in practice, experienced as clearly segregated, or separable from each other. Second, the passage from the real to the irreal need not always be materialized; it suffices, according to Sartre, that the perception of something on the background of the world involves, on the part of consciousness, the possibility of a double negation: that of denying that the thing belongs to the real, or that of denying the real in positing that thing (*IPPI* 183, 186). Third, the negation is never general, or arbitrary, in the sense that it is aimed at a particular thing (object, event or state-affairs) of which one negates particular aspects. Consciousness, for Sartre, does not hover over reality; it is always necessarily "situated in the world", being the directedness towards things (objects, events or states of affairs) from a particular (spatiotemporal, historical, moral, political, aesthetic or affective) standpoint (*IPPI* 185–7). The situatedness of consciousness means that in imagining, one "nihilates" particular things by negating specific aspects of them, forming a view of those things as being in certain respects different from how they are perceived. "Thus," Sartre insists, "the situation of consciousness must appear not as a pure and abstract condition of possibility for all of the imaginary, but as a concrete and precise motivation for the appearance of a certain particular imaginary" (*IPPI* 185).

Let us retrace the steps of the Sartrean argument so far. To imagine is to posit something as irreal; that is possible only against the background of things appearing at first as parts of the real world that is itself not a bare given, but the synthetic totality of things; the world can be constituted by consciousness because consciousness is free, that is, it is able to "stand back" and "surpass" the immediately given towards a meaningful whole, in perception, in action or in affection. When, in surpassing the given, one intends something as being different from how it is perceived as being, when one negates certain of its aspects, posited as real, one brings forth an "irreal" object: an object "withdrawn from reality". That "nihilation" of the object is always specific because it is motivated by the situation in which consciousness finds itself. And thus we reach the final important step in this reasoning.

"Constitution" and "nihilation" are the two essential moments of imagining activity. But, according to Sartre, who on this point remains an unrepentant Cartesian, constitution and nihilation are also the crucial moments of the activity through which consciousness reveals itself to itself:

> Is not the very first condition of the cogito doubt, which is to say the constitution of the real as a world at the same time as its nihilation from its same point of view, and does not the reflective grasp of doubt as doubt coincide with the apodictic intuition of freedom? (*IPPI* 186)

The question is rhetorical, and its objective is none other than to highlight the central place of imagination in the life of consciousness. Imagining is not an optional extra, it is not a rare charisma, or a contingent addition to our conscious engagement with the world. For Sartre, "imagination ... is the whole of consciousness as it realises its freedom" (*IPPI* 186).

In offering an account of the phenomena of imagination, Sartre (and I, along with him) appealed freely to a basic understanding of notions such as reality, essence and existence. It is time to look more closely at Sartre's mature analysis of those issues. The text that our discussion refers to will be the opening sections of Sartre's major philosophical treatise, *Being and Nothingness*.

CHAPTER SIX

Being

I

Being and Nothingness holds pride of place in Sartre's philosophical corpus. It is the culmination of a decade's involvement with phenomenological thought and sets the background for the moral, psychoanalytic, aesthetic and political propositions Sartre will articulate in the rest of his writing career. In between the methodological concerns that inform his early work, and the applied research that characterizes most of his later projects, there lies a text of substantial claims about the nature of being. The Greek word for "being" is *on* and the philosophical "discourse" or *logos* about being is *ontology*. Sartre conducts his ontological enquiry by adopting the standpoint of phenomenology, that is, by enquiring about being as it manifests itself. His analysis is closely attentive to the experience of what there is, providing a meticulous description of our encounter with being in perception, thought, feeling and action. That description purports to identify the basic structure of what there is, to analyse the grounds as well as the limits of our ability to affect how things are, and to illuminate the meaning of human conduct towards the world, towards oneself and towards others.

Given the foundational nature of an enquiry into being, and the wide scope of the Sartrean description of major types of experience of what there is, *Being and Nothingness* is a rich source of important ideas that pertain to most fields of philosophical research. Summarizing the results of the Sartrean enquiry would be no substitute for the study of a text whose main virtue lies not in the slogans that one might extract from it, but in the presentation of a detailed and thorough exploration of various philosophical paths towards an adequate understanding of reality. I shall, accordingly, focus on the part that presents some of the major difficulties for the reader who is unfamiliar with the basic aspects of Sartrean ontology. The fact that this part happens to be the "Introduction" to the whole book can often result in discouraging the further study of a work that begins with a chapter that is densely written in technical jargon, and which reads more like the conclusion to a long treatise than an invitation to a new philosophical project. It is hoped that the following sections will remove some of these difficulties by illuminating obscure points and by explicating certain lines of reasoning deployed in the "Introduction".

Our discussion will attend, rather closely, to particular points of Sartre's texts. It is my contention that those points do not necessarily express a neat philosophical doctrine. Sartre's governing aim in the opening part of the book is to convince the reader that some philosophical issues that are taken as settled are not really that happily resolved, and need to be reopened. Hence, instead of listing comprehensive answers, Sartre wishes to impress on the reader the need to reconsider some fundamental questions. Accordingly, his style is more aporetic than usual, and that will be reflected in our presentation, which will highlight some of the puzzles generated by a close reading of the Sartrean text.

II

Sartre introduces his ontological enquiry by posing a series of questions about being. His first question is about the extent to which contemporary philosophy has managed to rid itself of dualism. A dualistic approach is usually characterized by the division of reality into two regions of being, such as mental, abstract or spiritual, on the one hand, and bodily, concrete or material on the other. That is not the way "dualism" is understood in the present context. Sartre is interested not in the stuff of reality – what the world is made of – but in whether we can have a direct apprehension of reality for what it is, whether and how we can be aware of the world as it really is, whatever its stuff might be. The dualism under consideration is thus a doctrine about the nature of phenomena, and it contrasts the "exterior" appearance of objects to an "interior" essence that is forever hidden from view. At the time of writing *Being and Nothingness*, that dualism is considered defunct, and Sartre is happy to acknowledge the philosophical progress that has been made towards a non-dualistic, that is "monistic", view of appearances. Note, though, that Sartre does not argue for that view, but *from* it. He takes the monistic view of phenomena as given, clarifies its claims and probes its limitations for an adequate understanding of what there is. Let us see first what the monistic view states.

An appearance is nothing but a being appearing itself to the subject of experience. The being unfolds itself in a series of appearances, each of which forms part of a sequence of events whereby the being manifests itself to us. No single appearance can exhaust all aspects of a being, yet each of its appearances points not to something behind or above that being, but to the rest of its (past, contemporaneous and future) manifestations that form the series of its appearances. The concatenation of those appearances shows what something is and, in that sense, it reveals the thing's essence (*BN* 2; *EN* 5).[1]

The first thing to note about this account is that the identification of being with appearing is given from the standpoint of the latter. Sartre does not state that if something is a being then it appears; he asserts that if something appears then it is a being. This basic point is crucial for blocking a common misreading of the "Introduction" to *Being and Nothingness*; according to that reading, Sartre simply ventures some critical remarks with a view to elaborate or improve on the notion of phenomenon employed by previous phenomenologists. However, there is a sharp difference between Sartre and his predecessors on what we might call the *ontological point of entry* to phenomena; whereas they identify the real with what is in principle able to appear to us, Sartre is keen to emphasize the irreducibility of what there is to what is perceived or otherwise intended by us. Thus, his monistic view of the phenomenon affirms that that to which consciousness is directed is the being itself, and not "a superficial covering which hides from sight the true nature of the object" (*BN* 1). Yet, the identification of being with appearing is limited on two fronts. On the one hand, Sartre nowhere states that unless something appears, it does not exist. On the other hand, even when his discussion is limited to beings that do appear, his theory requires that "the being of that which *appears* does not exist *only* in so far as it appears" (*BN* 18; *EN* 29).

Another issue that arises with the way Sartre introduces his monistic view of phenomenon is that he seems to waver between the claim that the essence is given through the appearances and the claim that the essence is an appearance. The latter view seems the natural successor of Sartre's earlier discussions of perceptual objects as made out of the totality of their manifestations: "the object itself is the synthesis of all [its] appearances" (*IPPI* 8). However, that approach is quite problematic. First, it renders everything, even ordinary middle-sized material objects, as being forever beyond our grasp; if an object really were the synthesis of all its appearances to all possible observers occupying all possible points of view, then we would never be able to see, for example, a coffee cup as what it is. The problem with that approach is not that we cannot in principle see a cup from all possible viewpoints in the universe (that is of course true), but that unless we are able to do so we do not (and we should not) try to tell whether what we see is a cup or not: and that, to say the least, is a highly counter-intuitive conclusion.[2]

Second, that approach appears now to be resisted by Sartre himself. He writes that a physical reality is the synthetic unity of its manifestations, and that that unity is not the mere sum of all possible appearances, but a series governed by a "law", or a "principle", awareness of which equips us with the ability to know what an object is. That "law", or "principle", is that in virtue of which something is (appearing to be as) what it is and, in that sense, marks the essence of the perceived object (*BN* 2; *EN* 12).[3]

The new approach conceives of essence as different from, yet intimately related to, the appearances of a concrete object. However, in the same section Sartre also states that essence "is the concatenation of appearances; that is, itself an appearance" (*BN* 2; *EN* 12). If the claim simply reiterates the view that an appearance of the object shows the object itself, then it is consistent with the rest of the Sartrean doctrines. However, if the claim entails that the essence is one among the various aspects, sides or qualities of the object manifested in perception, then it is not clear to me that the claim coheres with Sartre's considered views on this matter. One way to achieve that coherence would be to think of "appearance" as a generic term for anything that stands before, or presents itself to, consciousness. Thus, a being manifests itself, through its various aspects, to our sense perception, while its essence appears to our intuition, understood as the activity in which an intentional object (be it abstract or concrete) is itself presented to consciousness. Sartre, in other words, is happy to subscribe to the possibility of *Wesenschau*, of the intuition of essence (*BN* 2; *EN* 12).[4]

In an important paragraph, Sartre notes that the appearing qualities of an object imply its essence, in the same way that "a sign implies its meaning" (*BN* 5; *EN* 15). Sartre is rather cryptic on the exact sense of "meaning" involved in this passage, but I suggest that we reconstruct his reasoning as follows. By showing (an aspect of) the object, each appearance reveals (part of the story of) what the object is. An appearance is a moment of an organized whole that presents itself to the subject as a particular kind of object, for example a coffee cup. However, that something is presented as a cup (as opposed to as a saucer or as a mug) depends on the subject's ability to see the series of appearances as appearances of the kind of object we think of as "cup". The appearances of the object point the subject in the direction of apprehending that object as being the particular object it is, that is, a cup. The appearances of the object refer (the subject) to the essence of the object. The essence is given to the subject through perception, in that from the appearances of the object the subject can determine what the essence of that object is. We can still talk of the "intuition of the essences" (*BN* 2; *EN* 12), albeit as an act *grounded on* the perception of the facing sides, aspects and qualities of the object, rather as an immediate perceptual grasp of the principle that unifies the appearances into one particular series. Indeed, it is not clear how a principle can be an object of perception, and Sartre does not provide a defence of such a claim. What he writes instead is that out of the qualities distinguished in the perceived object the subject may proceed to "determine an essence which [those qualities] imply" (*BN* 5; *EN* 15). Hence, the essence is not among the appearing sides or perceived qualities of the object but something implied by them. Admittedly, that implication does not constitute a passage from one kind of substance to another. Essence is not some other substance set beside or inside the perceived object. There is only one substance under consideration, namely the particular entity whose appearances "disclose" its essence as the "principle" of their series: or, in our terms, as that in virtue of which the object is the way it manifests itself as being.

We shall revisit the issue of essence later in the chapter. For the time being it suffices to bear in mind Sartre's fundamental commitment to the view that an appearance is not a substitute for a being, but the being itself appearing to us. Sartre employs the term "phenomenon" to capture the double character of appearance as both relative to a subject to whom it appears, and absolute in its appearance, since what a phenomenon is showing is not something beyond or behind it, but the being itself: "a phenomenon is ... *absolutely indicative of itself*" (*BN* 2; *EN* 12).

We might think at this stage that an appeal to phenomena should enable us to build a secure ontological theory that would deliver us from the problems besetting dualism. Sartre, however, goes on to raise some doubts about the success of that project. He shows that dualism dies hard; a doctrine that we seem to have left behind us in metaphysics is to make a comeback in the analysis of experience. Let us look at how Sartre argues for that view.

III

The perception of an object by a subject takes place at a particular point in space and time. In principle, as in practice, the same object can be perceived by the same subject from a different distance, or from a different angle, or at different times. The same applies for any point in time and space from which the object can be perceived by any subject suitably equipped by the relevant sense faculties. Each instance of perceiving an aspect of the object is finite, experienced by a particular subject at a specific spatiotemporal point; yet the very fact of perceiving an object implies the existence of a multiplicity of perceptual takes on that thing by the same or by other subjects, from that or different standpoints. Hence, the finite experience of looking at a cup goes hand in hand with the possibility of an infinite number of different perceivings of that cup, some of which might of course be actual when other people look simultaneously at different aspects of the cup, or when the same subject looks at the cup from a different angle, touches it in a different way, or hears the sound of its sides touched by a stirring teaspoon at different moments in time.

The duality of finite and infinite is not a contingent accompaniment of human experience; it constitutes one of its fundamental presuppositions. In ordinary circumstances, when I perceive a material object, for example a cup, I perceive it as real. The reality of that cup involves awareness that the cup "is there", and that "it is not me". How should we interpret the latter claim? By stating that how the object is, and has been, does not depend on what I think, fancy or dream about it. Even though the appearing cup is "relative to" me as a perceiver while one of its numerous aspects appears to me, the sequence of appearances of that cup is subject to a number of factors (such as the cup's material constitution and the role of physical, chemical, gravitational and other forces that determine the object's history), none of which "depends on my whim" (*BN* 2; *EN* 13). This point is not offered as a conclusion of a scientific theory, and does not require that the subject believes, or even that she is aware of, any such theory. Sartre's point is made exclusively on phenomenological grounds: what the cup I see looks like now is not *experienced by me as being* dependent on my likes or dislikes.[5] This important claim can be explored in a variety of ways. What is relevant for the present discussion is that the independence from the subject of the grounds that determine how something (is and, thus, how it) appears to the subject, implies that a finite perception of an aspect of the object from a particular spatiotemporal standpoint cannot fix the past, present and future appearances of the object whose number extends to infinity.

To appreciate the force of the above considerations, try to abstract from an actual perception of a cup and think of an appearance frozen in time: a complex of shapes and colours that now fills your visual field. If that appearance is to be anything more than a subjective plenitude in which your being is fully absorbed, your experience should move beyond the instantaneous presence of shapes and colours towards all those moments that make up the series of the cup's manifestations. To put it differently, if your finite experience is to be a perception of a transcendent natural object (i.e. an object that is encountered rather than made up by the experience), your experience has to transcend itself towards the series of appearances of that object at any one time and through time.

The appeal to phenomena enabled contemporary philosophy to shed away the metaphysical dualism of what is actually presenting itself to a subject and what is supposedly lurking behind the appearances as a mysterious power with the potential to run the life of a phenomenon behind the scenes. There are no real yet unrealized entities: everything there is, is actual.[6] However, the dualism of finite and infinite in the experience of objects brings with it a new version of traditional ontological distinctions. The object appears itself in each appearance as you are looking at a particular aspect of it from a particular point in space and time. Yet that appearance does not exhaust what the object is. To find that out you would have to grasp at once the total series of the object's appearances; but no experience can present to you simultaneously all aspects of an object for all possible manifestations of that object in time. What the object really is (its essence) lies constantly outside any one instant where the object presents itself to you (in its appearance). Hence, we recover a dualism of the particular appearance, as opposed to the total series of appearances that is already there, in each appearance, as the potentiality of transcending that appearance towards the total series of the manifestations of that object, that is, of the object's essence.

The interpretation of essence as the "principle" or "law" or "reason" of the series of manifestations of a being seems to limit, without however eliminating, the problem. A basic characteristic of imagined, or simply thought-of, objects is that they can be intuited for what they truly are with one mental act. To think of a cube, for instance, is to think of something defined by certain geometrical relations, but to acquire knowledge of a particular square object, on the other hand, we have – literally, no less than metaphorically – to make the tour of it: knowledge of its shape, size, colours or physical behaviour unfolds as we approach, handle and perceive that object in its different aspects from different perspectives. Hence, to know the principle that unifies the object we have to take on board a series of appearances so as to discover how and why the appearances form the particular series. Even if that series need not run to infinity, it might still extend beyond the finite takes on the object available to a particular subject. We are thus faced with a new version of the oppositions between the *inside* (the aspect *in* which the object is given) and the *outside* (the total series of the object's manifestations is not, and cannot, appear in any one aspect): of the *actuality* (of each one occurring manifestation) and the *potentiality* (of the infinite series of possible appearances); of *essence* (as the principle that governs a potentially infinite number of appearings) and *appearance* (as the, variously limited, single manifestation of the object).

We might expect, now, that Sartre will move the dialectic forwards by explicating the philosophical significance of the *recurrence* of the above oppositions. At a minimum, we would like Sartre to provide a clear yes or no to the question with which he opened the "Introduction": has modern thought's attempt to overcome a certain number of dualisms been successful? Instead, Sartre cuts that discussion short, and switches to another major issue concerning "the being of appearing". We shall see in a moment what that issue is. Let me suggest that the answer implied by Sartre's discussion is in the negative: modern philosophy has not succeeded in explaining away those oppositions. Their reappearance is indicative of the ineliminability of the distinction between inside and outside, potency and actuality, essence and appearance. Hence, a monistic worldview has to accommodate those oppositions, and to illuminate their role for human experience, instead of trying to ignore them.

A few pages into the book, Sartre has – in my view – achieved some preliminary, yet very important, results. He has shown that a correct understanding of phenomena presents us with direct access to how things are, without, though, eliminating a number of fundamental distinctions that inform our experience of reality. We have addressed how these distinctions relate a thing's essence. However, there we now need to examine the issue of "the being of" an object: not what it is, or why it is as it is, but the very fact that it is. In other words we have to talk about existence.[7]

IV

"Being" has acquired a lofty status in theoretical debates, but in ordinary discourse the word is used as the present tense participle of the verb "to be": "being on holiday" means that one is on holiday, and "being around" means that one is around. If we remove the adjectives from the previous phrases, we are left with the meaning of "being" as "existing". Adding the definite article "the" to the participle "being" turns the latter into a noun that can refer to the existence of something. "The being of a phenomenon" can refer to what a phenomenon is, or to the fact that a phenomenon exists. Sartre poses a preliminary question for his ontology, which exploits the meaning of "being" in a fruitful way; he enquires whether the being of phenomenon is the same as the phenomenon of being (*BN* 4; *EN* 14).

To answer that question properly, we need to understand first what it means. The "phenomenon of being" refers to the appearance of being to us, and, thus, to our experience of being, or, in other words, to our experience of existence. Existence appears to us, in the sense that we have an awareness of it that enables us to think or talk about it. That awareness does not necessarily amount to knowledge. Indeed, Sartre affirms that the ordinary awareness of existence is very different from the construction of theories, or the forming of judgements, about existence. What matters for Sartre, at this point, is the ordinary pre-reflective apprehension of existence: that is, the subjective pole of the appearance of existence. The "phenomenon of being" is the event whereby *being*, in the sense of *existing*, appears to us.

The "being of the phenomenon", on the other hand, concerns what a phenomenon is. What defines something as a phenomenon is that it appears itself to a subject. The appearing of the object is what is essential about that object *as* a phenomenon. Hence, the initial way to understand Sartre's question is as asking whether all there is to the existence of objects is that those objects appear to us. And his answer is a resounding no. The being of particular objects – their existing – is not equivalent to the fact that they appear to us – their being phenomena. Sartre employs the term "transphenomenal" in order to express the fact that being of an object is not exhausted in its appearing, and thus, that it "*trans*cends" the "*phenomenal*".

Traditionally, philosophers would jump from a claim of non-coincidence between existence and appearance to a doctrine of radical separation of things as they appear to our senses from things as they really are. Sartre's move is very different. It is because he believes that a phenomenon is the object appearing itself for what it is that he denies that existence reveals itself as one among the object's features. Try to consider the opposite view that, *pace* Sartre, existence could appear as one among the features of the object, for example as a quality, a part, a relation or a signification of the object. Existence is not a perceptible quality of the object next to its size or volume: to be sure, if a chest of drawers exists, it exists as an object of a certain height, depth, weight or colour and its existence is the existence of all those qualities equally. However, existence is not among the dimensions of the object but a presupposition for the object having any dimensions in the first place. Existence is not a part that belongs to, or is possessed by, the object: it is not like one of the drawers that belongs to a piece of furniture. And to be informed that there is a chest of drawers next door is not like being told that a chest of drawers that had three drawers has now acquired a fourth. Existence is not, cannot be reduced to, a relation of the object to something else. It might be true of an existing object that is a certain distance from the door and adjacent to the wall. However, it is because it exists that it lies, for example, half a metre from the door, and not because there is a "half a metre distance" from the door that an object exists. Finally, Sartre asserts that existence is not something "signified" by the object. We may interpret that claim as pointing to a sharp distinction between the existential and the predicative senses of the verb "to be". Sartre rejects the view that the existential sense of "being" can be reduced to a predicative sense, because for any predicate chosen its opposite is equally implying existence, rather than the opposite of existence. Sartre considers and rejects the (seemingly plausible, but ultimately misleading) identification of "being" with "presence", on the grounds that "absence" is equally revealing of the object's existence (*BN* 5; *EN* 15); learning that Peter is absent from the meeting does not entail that there is no such being as Peter, since you cannot "be absent" without "being" in the first place. One might retort that, regarding existence, "absence" is on a par with "presence" only if the absent entity is present somewhere else; one might thus claim that to exist is just to be present somewhere. In response, we should accept the claim that, in certain contexts, "being" and "being present" are coextensive. However, even if that claim were correct, the objection takes things the wrong way round: something is (present) at a particular place because (among other things) it exists, but it does not exist because it is (present) in that particular place.[8]

There is a further way, though, to interpret the Sartrean statement that "the [perceived] object does not refer to being as to a signification" (*BN* 5; *EN* 15). A signification is what is signified, or meant by an object. But an object cannot mean or signify its existence, since it would be futile to address myself to the object in order to apprehend its being.[9] The Sartrean approach to this issue is markedly different from an ontological project that would purport to effect a revelation of being by interrogating the existence of particular objects by positing, for instance, about a coffee cup, the question of what it means to exist.[10] The phenomenological problem with such a project is twofold. First, the moment we focus on what it is (or even, on what it means) to be, the concrete object vanishes from view, swallowed by the overarching puzzle of the meaning of "the being of beings". Thus, contrary to its proclaimed method, that approach undermines the primacy of the phenomenology of the experience of concrete objects, for an intellectualist, or, at least, reflective apprehension of existence that should allegedly ground our ordinary awareness of existents. Second, by positing being as something revealed to us, our relation to it becomes subject to the rules pertaining to the experience of phenomena. Hence, being is rendered to an appearance that "as such, needs in turn a being on the basis of which it can reveal itself" (*BN* 5; *EN* 15).[11]

All in all, existence does not appear as a quality, a possession or a signification of the object. Should we, then, conclude that existence is hidden by the object? Sartre says not: the object does not hide existence, "for it would be futile to try to push aside certain qualities of the existent" in order to find the existence behind them (*BN* 5; *EN* 15). Furthermore, Sartre affirms that there is something that the object signifies, but this is not its "being" in the sense of its existence, but its "being" in the sense of (that in virtue of which the object is) "what it is": the object points to its essence as the "meaning" of its various manifestations.

We are thus faced with the following puzzle. We are aware of existence (there is a phenomenon of being), yet the objects we encounter manifest to us *what* they are, but not *that* they are (they do not refer to their existence in the way they refer to their essence). For Sartre, the solution to the puzzle lies in the fact that existence is not an item revealed by the object, but the condition of the revelation of the object (*BN* 5; *EN* 15). The key to that solution is offered by the contrast drawn between conceptual understanding, on the hand, and immediate access, on the other. Conceptual understanding aspires to knowledge of what something really is: it focuses on the various aspects, properties or relations of the object, and it purports to identify, explain and characterize an object for what it is – its essence. Existence, on the other hand, appears to us without conceptual intermediaries, as it can make its presence felt directly, in moments of boredom (*ennui*) or nausea. The narration of how the world is lived by the subject in those moments becomes an important part of ontological enquiry; and, as we know, such a narration has been undertaken by Sartre in the form of the novel – the only discursive form that can do justice to the elusive yet overwhelming character of the relevant experiences (*BN* 4; *EN* 14).

V

It appears to me that, despite its undeniable appeal, the above analysis bequeaths to Sartrean ontology a few problems. A first problem concerns the notion of being as the "condition of every revelation". Conditions, in contrast to the phenomenon or the event that they condition, are not immediately available to the perceiving subject; rather, they need to be somehow extracted, or inferred, through appropriate analysis of the phenomenon that they make possible. One problem, therefore, is how this inferential status of being is related to the alleged immediacy of the experience of being that we noted at the end of the previous section. Furthermore, given Sartre's well-motivated preference for thinking of conditions as "transcendental", it becomes even harder to see how being as the "condition of every revelation" can be offered to the "revealing intuition of the phenomenon of being" (*BN* 5; *EN* 15). A transcendental condition is just not the kind of thing that can be the object of immediate, lived experience, not least because, as Sartre himself had convincingly shown in *The Transcendence of the Ego*, a transcendental condition is not a thing (*TE* 2–3).

The need to address the above worry might partly explain an otherwise arbitrary move in Sartre's argumentation. In the paragraph where he talks about being as the condition of every revelation, Sartre notes that as soon as I pass beyond a particular entity toward its being, being becomes "an appearance which as such, needs in turn a being on the basis of which it can reveal itself" (*BN* 5; *EN* 15). That claim might sound right, but Sartre offers here no reason in its support. What makes the appearing of *being* (in the sense of existence) dependent on *a* being (an existent)?

A similar move occurs later in the chapter where Sartre affirms that securing the being of any attitude requires that we ground that attitude on a being; he writes, for instance, that "the known [should refer us] to the knowledge and knowledge to the being that knows" (*BN* 7; *EN* 17). Once more, I believe Sartre to be right on this point, but his being right does not release him from the obligation to argue for it. The question is: why is *connaître* dependent on *un être connaissant*? What makes an activity or a process dependent on a being, that is, on something that belongs to a different ontological category? And, more generally but closer to our concerns: why is *être* dependent for its revelation on *un être*?

My suggested answer is that the dependence in question offers a way out of the impasse we identified earlier. Existence as a (transcendental) condition is not available to be experienced; it becomes so only on the basis of an existent that is open to our experience. *Being* is thus dependent on *a* being in order to appear. In order to clarify this point (or, perhaps, in order to make things even more complicated), Sartre warns that "it is characteristic of the being of an existent to not reveal itself, in person, to consciousness" (*BN* 18; *EN* 29). And part of the explanation for this necessarily incomplete availability of being to consciousness points back to Sartre's allusion to being as a "condition" . The term employed now is "foundation": "being is the ever present foundation of the existent", since "there is no being which is not the being of a certain mode of being" (*BN* 18; *EN* 29).[12] Let us try to unpack the significance of that claim.

VI

The paragraph in which the above phrases appear comes from the final section of the "Introduction", entitled "The Being-in-itself". Sartre employs that expression by way of contrast to the mode of being that is necessarily and wholly presence to itself, called "being-for-itself", that is the mode of being of consciousness.[13] Recall consciousness's "duty" to be a "revealing revealed": revealed *to* itself *as* the revealing intuition of the appearing objects (*BN* 9).[14] On the contrary, the being of object is open neither to itself nor to consciousness; at least, it is not wholly available to consciousness, even while the object manifests itself in its perceptible aspects (*BN* 18).[15] The being of that which appears is not exhausted in its appearing. The being of a phenomenon (of an object in its appearing) is "transphenomenal": it transcends the phenomenal condition, because "it does not exist only in so far as it appears" (*BN* 18; *EN* 29).

Given the contrastive way in which the notion of being-in-itself is introduced, it is common for most scholars to proceed with their interpretation by focusing on the particulars of the distinction drawn by Sartre between being-in-itself and being-for-itself. Weighing the pros and cons of the wealth of interpretations offered for the final section of the "Introduction" eventually requires debating on the argumentative coherence of *Being and Nothingness*, and that is beyond the scope of this chapter.[16]

Instead, I should like to close this discussion by addressing an issue that somehow precedes that of assessing the exact relation between being-in-itself and being-for-itself. The issue is rather simple but, to my mind, quite puzzling: what could a *mode of being* possibly be?

Before we venture an answer, it is important to appreciate the source of the puzzle. The expression "modes of being" purports to signify different ways of existing. Sartre asserts that there are two major ways of existing. What he fails to explicate is how existence can come in different ways, or manners, or modes. Perhaps Sartre felt no need to proffer such an explication, given that the doctrine of the multiplicity of modes of being is shared by a few major philosophers of the recent and the distant past, including some who had a significant presence in his thinking. However, that explication is, I think, outstanding, since the doctrine in question is, to my mind, false. Moreover, it is false for reasons that can be derived from Sartre's own discussion. Let me explain.

To be is to exist. To claim of a table (or a concept, or a flying horse), that it is, is to claim of it that it exists (cf. "*être* (existentia)" [*EN* 21]). For Sartre, everything that is, "even as unreal it must exist" (*BN* 15).[17] A particular table (or concept, or flying horse) does not exist "a little", or "a lot" (existence is not a matter of quantity), nor "weakly" or "forcefully" (existence is not a matter of intensity): it either exists or it does not. Existence, as we have also seen, is not a quality, a part, a relation or a signification of the object (see *BN* 5). Most importantly, though, existence is not some kind of activity, something performed by an existent; but if it is not an activity, then it cannot enjoy a *way*, or a *mode*, or a *manner* in which it is supposedly performed. Indeed, existence is not any kind of *event* (a particular, datable occurrence consisting in changes in the properties or relations of a persisting existent); but if it is not an event it cannot enjoy a *way*, or a *mode*, or a *manner* in which it supposedly unfolds.[18]

I would suggest that talk of "ways, modes or manners of being" is something Sartre uncritically, but to my mind unnecessarily, inherited from philosophers he justly admired. His luminous discussion of being and of nothingness can proceed without a commitment to those particular turns of phrase. Moreover, Sartre's alternative phrase of "regions of being" is more apposite, involves him in fewer conceptual problems, and is in harmony with his commitment to a notion of being as such, of "*being* in general" (*BN* 23; *EN* 33). However, we shall not pursue any of those constructive (a kinder word than "revisionary") ideas here. Instead, it might be of more benefit to the reader to try to identify some possible objections to my interpretation.

I can think of three main challenges to my critique. The first is: granted, existence is not an activity – but it can be some kind of *passivity* which characterizes essentially being in itself. The response to that objection can be found in Sartre's own masterful argumentation for the claim that the notion of passivity is misapplied not just to perceiving consciousness, but also, and primarily, to the being of the objects perceived (*BN* 13–15; *EN* 24–6). In a nutshell, Sartre's point is that passivity requires the form of contact that enables the being of the item at the receiving end to be affected by the being of the item at the active end; but no such form of contact is available among a thing and the no-thing that consciousness is: "The perceived thing is in front of consciousness; consciousness cannot reach it, and it can not enter into consciousness; and as the perceived being is cut off from consciousness, it exists cut off from its own existence" (*BN* 15; *EN* 26).

The second objection is: being-for-itself is constantly engaging in a number of activities, such as negating, perceiving, imagining, thinking, nihilating and so on. Consciousness, after all, is necessarily always consciousness *of* something, and it would cease to exist the moment it stopped engaging in some form of intentional activity. Thus, when it comes to the being-for-itself of consciousness, it is all too reasonable to talk about *modes*, or *ways*, or *manners*.

In a sense, all those claims are correct, but they are beside the point. Sartre believes that a consciousness deprived of intentionality is an impossibility, and, hence, a consciousness that would cease intending anything would cease to exist. But he does not assert that among the various intentional activities in which consciousness engages is that of existing! I think that the closest he comes to considering that issue in the "Introduction'" is in his discussion of the determination of consciousness by itself. Yet, even there he warns that such "self-determination" should not be mistaken for some kind of act or event, through which consciousness somehow is bringing itself into existence: "This determination of consciousness by itself must not be conceived as a genesis, as a becoming, ... as an act" (*BN* 11; *EN* 21–2). To put the point in simpler terms, it might be true to claim of being-for-itself that it constantly does things, as it is true to assert that being-for-itself cannot do anything unless it exists; but that does not entail that one of the things it does is to exist.

A third objection would go as follows: talk of *modes of being* signifies a difference that pertains to what we might call the ontological order. All things are beings, but, depending on their ontological category, they enjoy or exemplify a different mode of being. Given the vast variety of things "on heaven and earth", Sartre's talk of different modes of being is a way to introduce the important distinction among things that *are*, things that *subsist*, and things that *exist*.

The response to that objection can be brief. Nowhere in the "Introduction" does Sartre draw such a distinction. There is nothing in his argumentation that invokes as a premise claims of the form "consciousness *subsists*, while what it is conscious of *exists*", or "consciousness *exists*, while what its activity brings forth only *is*", or, indeed, any claim that would employ such jargon. That is not a mere stylistic choice. Rather, it relates to Sartre's conviction that it would be wrong to approach "the concrete, that is man within the world" (*BN* 27; *EN* 37–8) by assuming that any of its integral moments (e.g. the being-in-itself, the being-for-itself and the being-for-others), has lesser existence than the others.

Notes

1. A narrative prelude

1. Work on the themes of the novel dates back to 1928, and most of the views expressed in the text precede the writings on phenomenology that will occupy Sartre during the 1930s; cf. Contat & Rybalka (1970).
2. "[Ç]a représente … la mise en forme d'une idée philosophique … Si je ne l'avais pas rendue sous cette forme romanesque, l'idée n'était pas encore assez solide pour que j'en fasse un livre philosophique" (*OR* 1699–1700).
3. The original reads "pour y voir clair" (*OR* 6). The 1963 Penguin translation renders this "in order to understand" (*N* 9).
4. At least, they do not exist according to the story told in *Nausea*; for a very different approach, see *BN* 18–19; *EN* 29. For an analysis of existence in *Being and Nothingness*, see Chapter 6, §VI.
5. The differences between *Nausea* and *Being and Nothingness* in the description of temporal experience is a further point of tension between the two works, and seriously undermines a practice common to many Sartrean scholars of using the later treatise as an explication manual for the early novel; for some expressions of that view see the otherwise invaluable commentaries Barnes (1959), Fletcher (1968), Goldthorpe (1968), Edwards (1971).
6. For a recent example of this reading see James Wood's overall problematic "Editor's Introduction" to *Nausea* (Wood 2000: vii–viii).
7. Some classic statements of this approach include Murdoch (1953), Barnes (1959), Edwards (1971); for a seminal critique of these views, see Spanos (1978).

2. Intentionality

1. The exact dating of Sartre's first article in phenomenology has been a subject of dispute among scholars. Vincent de Coorebyter has argued convincingly, to my mind, that the original draft dates back to Sartre's first systematic study of Husserl's views during his sojourn in Berlin, in 1933–34; cf. Coorebyter (2000: 27–9).
2. What about the subject of consciousness? Is this not a "thing" included in the experience? Strictly speaking, no. As we shall see in Chapter 3, Sartre affirms that

attending to the event of the consciousness of an object, we do not find a subject lurking anywhere; talk about a "subject of experience" might make its appearance only at the level of reflecting on, or offering a metaphysical account of, that experience, neither of which is part of the first-order, ordinary and pre-reflective consciousness of things in the world; cf. esp. Chapter 3, §II.

3. As we shall see later, the (reflected) consciousness can become the object of (reflecting) consciousness, without ceasing to affirm its own intentional object. Therefore, even in its reflective moments, conscious activity requires an object on which it is directed, and which is other than consciousness itself; cf. Chapter 3, §IV for detailed defence and discussion.
4. For a classic statement of this view see Brentano (1955: 88), and see Brandl (2005) for a qualified defence of the immanentist theory of intentionality.
5. For the second approach see Sartre's critical remarks on Husserl's theory of intentionality in his first treatise on imagination, *L' Imagination* (*Ion* 144–5). The question of whether Husserl himself subscribed to an immanentist theory of intentionality is addressed well by Drummond (2003).
6. See Robert Sokolowski's lucid description of that experience (2000: ch. 2).
7. Kelly (2003) makes several insightful remarks on this problem.
8. Hence I think that the translation of "*faces*" as "aspects" in the new English edition of *L'Imaginaire* is really apposite. It also shows the Sartrean approach to be hospitable to the view that it is part of our experience of spatiotemporal entities, that objects somehow "face" or "see" each other from points of view not available to an observer (and, thus, that the hidden-to-an-observer aspect of a lamp might be the facing-the-armchair aspect of the lamp). That view is developed by Merleau-Ponty ([1945] 1962: 68). To be sure, Sartre could only take such talk metaphorically, given his belief that only conscious beings can be present to something and thus, only such beings can see or face worldly objects, or each other; see *BN* III, ch. 2, §i.
9. Cf. *TE* 51 for Sartre's view that only a phenomenological approach – cleared from any idealist prejudices – can respect, and thus offer, a valid analysis of "the resistance of things".
10. Note in this connection Sartre's cautious adoption of the notions of "data" or of "sensation" in *L'Imagination*, ch. 4. Sartre is keen to emphasize that such items (if they exist) cannot appear as objects, but, at most, as that through which consciousness intends its objects, either in perception or in imagination, possibly by animating an otherwise inert given (see *Ion* 145). Therefore, in that work, sensations can figure as part of an immanent content, which should be sharply distinguished from the intentional object. We take up this issue in more detail, below, in Chapter 5, esp. §III and §V.
11. Here, as in the following section, I refer to particular paragraphs from the introductory chapter of *Being and Nothingness*, paragraphs that illuminate some basic conceptual issues that run through Sartre's early philosophical work. In my view, the "Introduction" in *Being and Nothingness* serves the dual role of giving an accurate account of the theoretical commitments that inform much of "*pensée moderne*" up to that moment (including Sartre's own early work), while bringing into the open the internal tensions and conceptual limitations of that early work in dealing with some crucial ontological issues. In its former constructive aspect, it helps the presentational aims of our discussion; regarding its latter, self-critical aspect, see my remarks in Chapter 6.
12. Hereafter, when we talk about the perceptual presentation of an object, our discussion focuses on the case that preoccupies Sartre in his philosophical writings,

that is the case of *visual* perception (I am grateful to Jonathan Webber for pressing me on this point). Whether the analysis of sight provides the right model for understanding the other senses is a crucial and not easily resolvable issue. That issue has important ramifications not only for the accurate interpretation of, for example, tactile or auditory experience, but also for the justifiability of philosophical attempts (including those of Sartre) to portray awareness of abstract objects, in logic or mathematics, on the lines of visual perception (cf. Chapter 3, §II). For discussion of the relation between visual perception and other sense modalities see Hurley & Noë (2003), Fish (2010: esp. ch. 9); on auditory experience see Nudds (2001); and on touch Martin (1992). On that issue, as well as on several others pertaining to the phenomenology of sense experience, with allusions to views of both Husserl and Sartre, the most thorough discussion is still Merleau-Ponty ([1945] 1962: pt I).

13. See especially the discussion of imagination in Chapter 5, §§V–VII.
14. See, for instance, *IPPI* 8–12. Husserl famously distinguishes between "the object, such as it is intended, and the object pure and simple, which is intended" (1913: 579); cf. Drummond (2003: 90).
15. See Dan Zahavi's fine overview of these notions from a Husserlian standpoint (Zahavi 2003: 23–7).
16. That is a view of content eloquently supported by Tim Crane's (2001) analysis, and elaborated further in Crane (2003).
17. "Percevoir c'est buter contre une presence" (1981b; reprinted in *Situations IV* [1964: 197]).
18. This is an error that will be addressed in Chapter 4, from §III.

3. The ego

1. Among several authors pursuing that line of interpretation, Gennaro (2002), Kriegel (2003), Schroeder (2004) and Wilford (2006) offer the most systematic defence and discussion.
2. For a clear statement of that interpretation see Wider (1997: 41ff.).
3. My modal understanding of attention comes in direct contrast to a faculty-based approach, according to which there is a higher-order psychological faculty of attention, to which the lower-order faculties of observing, listening and so on are subordinated; cf. Christopher Peacocke's (1998) influential articulation of that view in. However, my point regarding the disanalogy between positional and attentive consciousness is not affected by the particulars of the currently thriving debate over the nature of attention.
4. Let me note, again, that the distinction between "non-focal" and "non-attentive" is required for cases where what one visually focuses on (e.g. the computer screen in front of him) may not be what he is paying attention to (e.g. the loud voices coming from the flat above).
5. I would be happy to grant, though, that the notion of "non-positional" can be usefully introduced to the uninitiated, not by identifying it with peripheral vision, but by using peripheral vision as an example of being aware of something on which one is not focused.
6. In one of the most careful discussions of this problem, Stephen Priest notes optimistically that the dependence of consciousness on the object, and of the object on consciousness might be overcome (*Aufgehoben*) in the Hegelian sense of the

term. Assuming that such overcoming is feasible within Hegelian logic, it is highly questionable how it relates at all to Sartre's own approach to these issues. See Priest (2000: ch. 3), and Chapter 3, §V.

7. I would thus share Coorebyter's (2000) critique of scholars who claim to find in *The Transcendence of the Ego* the claim that the body individuates consciousness, while I have doubts over his view that Sartre's philosophical argumentation could be actually complete without bringing the body into the discussion.
8. The major issue here, of course, is how Sartre reads Husserl's later works; cf. Coorebyter (2000) for an evaluation of Sartre's understanding of constitutive phenomenology; cf. also the issue of deep self in Sarah Richmond's (2007) insightful analysis, as well as Bard (2002: ch. 3).

4. Emotion

1. In the 1930s, the psychology of emotions was already counting several decades of empirical research. For an early attempt at philosophical systematization of the relevant findings see Ribot's *Psychologie des Sentiments* (1896).
2. Clean versions of each doctrine are hard to find, but for cognitivist accounts see Neu (2000), Nussbaum (2001), Solomon (2003); for physiologically orientated ones see Damasio (1999), Carruthers (2000) and Prinz (2004).
3. We should stress here the important (yet often neglected) distinction between intra-personal balance, highlighted by Sartre, and interpersonal conflicts, underlined by contemporary theorists on the practical rationality of emotions, such as Paul Griffiths (2003).
4. Cf. the conciliatory remarks on the reality of feelings ventured by judgementalists such as Martha Nussbaum (2001) and Robert Solomon (2003).
5. See Hannah Pickard's (2003) elaborate attempt to effect that identification.
6. The "as-if loop" of emotionally related brain activity is explored by Antonio Damasio (1999), and discussed by Jesse Prinz (2004).
7. For various lists of basic emotions see Ekman (1980), Griffiths (2003), and Prinz (2004).
8. *STE* 17–26 discusses a functionalist development of Pierre Janet's psychodynamic theory of psychaesthenic conduct; cf. Janet (1909, 1927).
9. This paragraph highlights the issue on which Sartre disagrees with Gestalt psychology. However, the work of Gestalt psychologists plays an important role in the formation of Sartre's own theory of emotion since it facilitates the Sartrean move of presenting emotion as a form of altering the shape of a situation by effecting changes not on the world but on oneself.
10. Such an attack will be deployed a few years later, most notably in *Being and Nothingness*. However, even in that work the criticism of the unconscious serves the purpose of clarifying particular aspects of human conduct; see *BN* I, ch. 2.
11. In what follows I present Sartre's account of Freudian psychoanalysis. Two provisos are therefore in order. First, Sartre's account does not *ipso facto* give us an accurate understanding of Freud's theory. Second, Freud's theory is not the only way to develop the psychoanalytic approach to emotional phenomena. The discussion of those issues is well beyond the concerns of this book. However, I make some remarks on the first point during my evaluation of the Sartrean interpretation below. On the second point the reader will find particularly useful the work on psychoanalytic meta-theory by Betty Cannon (1993).

12. The phenomenon of therapeutic resistance is nicely brought out in *BN* pt I, ch. 2, §i.
13. For the possibility of an alternative, existentially informed psychoanalytic practice, see *BN* pt IV, ch. 2, §ii.
14. Sartre illustrates this point by noting disapprovingly that, according to classical psychoanalysis, "a pincushion in a dream always signifies a woman's breast, entry into a carriage signifies the sexual act" (*STE* 33). However, if I understand him correctly, the main problem Sartre finds with classical psychoanalysis is not that the connections it sets have always the same relata, but that they are supposed to overdetermine the conscious activity of human agents.
15. See Richard Wollheim's remarks on Janet and Freud (Wollheim 1991: ch. 8).
16. Cf. Jonathan Lear's (2005: 27) fine discussion on the importance of naming a preconscious state.
17. The conceptual issues raised by the experience of emotions that seem to resist cognitive control is thoroughly addressed by Justin D'Arms and Daniel Jacobson (2003).
18. Cf. Wollheim's (1991) concise and insightful reconstruction of the psychoanalytic view on this point. Wollheim talks about "idea" and "affect", however, the notion of mental content is I think more apposite given, on the one hand, the philosophical equivocity of the term idea, and the Freudian emphasis on mental states as "representations".
19. That line of reasoning can help us reconstruct the epistemology of emotion encountered both in psychoanalytically minded philosophers, such as John Deigh (1996), and those who are straightforwardly judgmentalist, such as Solomon (2003) and Nussbaum (2001).
20. Craig DeLancey directly invokes alexithymia in this context. See DeLancey (2002) for a very clear and systematic discussion of this issue.
21. For presentation of the relevant experimental work on alexithymia, interpreted as a clinical condition associated with a range of medical diagnoses, such as post-traumatic stress disorder, anorexia nervosa or Asperger's syndrome, see the pioneering work of Peter Sifneos (1972) and Richard Lane *et al.* (1996).
22. I employ DeLancey's formulation in order to attack his defence of unconscious emotion that invokes precisely those two inabilities (DeLancey 2002: 13–14).
23. See LeDoux (1984) and Zajonc (1984) for the experiments; Zajonc *et al.* (1989) and DeLancey (2002) for the relevant interpretation.
24. I have used the neutral expression "received as a danger" instead of "conceived" or "perceived", because the latter two can be taken to imply cognitive activities that can be absent from the phenomenon under consideration.
25. See Öhman & Soares (1994) and Esteves *et al.* (1994). Robert Zajonc's work is an important source of methodological and theoretical considerations on conducting experiments that induce a certain range of emotion-related responses; Zajonc (1984).
26. Cf. Peter Goldie's remarks on this point (Goldie 2000: ch. 1).
27. This is a point, I think, granted even by contemporary supporters of the James–Lange approach, such as Prinz (2004: chs 2, 4); cf. Hatzimoysis (2003a).
28. "Emotion is a specific way of apprehending the world" (*STE* 35).
29. It will help a lot to keep in mind that basic conception of "magic" when we come to consider the question of the internal consistency of Sartre's account of emotion, towards the end of this chapter.
30. For some important discussions of this issue see Hursthouse (1991), Smith

(1998), Goldie (2000), DeLancey (2002), Döring (2003), Helm (2010) and Tappolet (2010).

31. This is a view consistently discussed and defended by Sartre; see esp. *STE* 36–8, *BN* III, ch. 2, §i.
32. Richmond (2010) is required reading on this topic for the acuteness with which it addresses that issue, identifies its sources and makes a case for the superiority of the late over the early account given in the *Sketch for a Theory of the Emotions*.
33. The literature over the so-called "moral realism" debate and its bearing on the philosophical conception of emotions is vast; cf. Sayre-McCord (1988), Darwall *et al.* (1997) and Hatzimoysis (2003d) for some discussion; Dancy (1993) nicely shows how certain Cartesian assumptions about the objective world find their counterpart in Humean accounts of the subjective mind.
34. Cf. "A world – that means individual syntheses in mutual relations and possessing *qualities*" (*STE* 54).
35. "[T]he physiological phenomena … represent the genuineness of the emotion, they are the phenomena of belief" (*STE* 50).
36. The "captivity" involved is not without the possibility of resolution that stems either from reality itself, or from a reflexive turn of consciousness: "Liberation can come", albeit "only from a purifying reflection or from a total disappearance of the emotional situation" (*STE* 53).

5. Imagining

1. I should note that the philosophical neglect of imagination is by no means a sin just of the past. The recent, authoritative *A Companion to Phenomenology and Existentialism* (Dreyfus & Wrathal 2006) contains not a single entry on imagination, not even in the subject index.
2. Sartre's reference to "psychology" is reminiscent of Husserl's term "descriptive psychology' for the descriptive branch of phenomenological analysis of consciousness.
3. In §IX we shall examine how these considerations have a bearing on the problem of the "illusion of immanence".
4. Cf. in this connection Sartre's reference to the representative element in images "shot through with the flow of creative will" (*IPPI* 15).
5. See, for an exception, Casey (2000), who discusses similar issues at length, although not in connection with the specifics of the Sartrean analysis.
6. For good discussions of memory from a phenomenological perspective, see Marbach (1993) and Sokolowski (2000).
7. I characterize it as the "standard" and not the "exclusive" procedure of the first part, because it is not the only kind of evidence Sartre is using in that part (he is also looking at the behavioural and material substrate of the phenomena that constitute the "image family"), whereas it is also a procedure employed, to a lesser extent, in all the other parts of his treatise.
8. For that reason it would be inaccurate to maintain that *The Imaginary* launches a "devastating criticism on scientific psychology", as claimed on the cover of the recent (otherwise excellent) English edition of *L' Imaginaire*. Sartre appeals to the evidence of experimental psychology, and is not averse to conducting basic experiments of his own when he needs to pose some empirical challenge to his interpretative hypotheses.

9. That is, I think, in a nutshell the point of the second section of *The Imaginary*, pt I, entitled "The Image is a Consciousness".
10. The interpretation of Sartre as eliminativist is put forward, albeit cautiously, by Eric Lormand (2006), who links Sartre to Michael Tye (1995) and Ned Block (1983). Lormand offers several interesting remarks on the metaphysics of image to which we shall return when we address the question of the illusion of immanence in later sections.
11. In his earlier treatise on the subject, *L'Imagination* (1936), Sartre maintains a critical distance from attempts to downplay the reality of imaginative experiences, draws an interesting parallel between J. B. Watson's behaviourist approach and F. Moutier's dismissal of images, and is rather strict in his critique of Alain's approach, which bears significant resemblance to contemporary eliminativist doctrines (see esp. *Ion* 129–32).
12. This is a doctrine implied by some eliminativist views; cf. Block's remarks, reported in Lormand (2006).
13. Sartre appears to accept as much in noting: "to tell the truth, the expression 'mental image' gives rise to confusion … as the word 'image' is long-standing, we cannot reject it completely. But to avoid all ambiguity, I repeat here that an image is nothing other than a relation" (*IPPI* 7).
14. In §IX we shall discuss how, according to Sartre, awareness of the eye movement might partly explain the philosophical mystery surrounding the constitution of mental images (*IPPI* 73–82).
15. See, for instance, O'Shaughnessy (2002) on propositional imagining, and Casey (2000: 42–4, 15–16) on imagining-that and hypothesizing.
16. "The imaging consciousness … will seek its object on the ground of perception and aims at the sensitive elements that constitute the object" (*IPPI* 15).
17. Hence Sartre's claim that it is at most a quasi-observation (*IPPI* 10).
18. Cf. Bolzano (1837: I, 304), Moore (1966: 119ff.), Crane (2001: 22–34); cf. Drummond (2003) for an important discussion of those issues.
19. *Ion* ch. 4, discusses content in the context of Husserlian phenomenology.
20. For Sartre's use of the "animation" metaphor see *IPPI* 28, 41, 127.
21. For the importance of outline shape in the resemblance theory of depiction, see Hopkins (1998: ch. 3).
22. Lormand (2006) offers a lucid discussion of this matter. He discusses and rejects some standard candidates of "mental likenesses of imagined physical objects, entities with some of the perceptible properties as what's imagined" (*ibid.*: 317).
23. Cf. Jonathan Webber's instructive remarks in his "Introduction" to *The Imaginary* (*IPPI* xvii).
24. Cf. *inter alia*, the criticisms articulated by Warnock (1970), Kearney (1998) and Casey (2000).
25. Cf. in this regard, Hopkins's important discussion (1998: ch. 7).
26. This "ought to" is practical, encompassing all forms of human agency, and is not limited to the so-called "moral ought". The view presented here is enriched and elaborated in *BN* pt IV.

6. Being

1. Cf. "Essence is everything we can indicate … with the words – that is" (*BN* 59).
2. One may reasonably wonder whether that point can be undercut by noting that

our view of something as a cup may be justified not by having seen all possible profiles of it but instead by its being most likely to be a cup given the profiles we have seen. However, if the identity of an object were determined by *all* – not just by some, already perceived – of its appearances, Sartre would be right to insist that the problem remains. (Thanks to Jonathan Webber for raising this point.)

3. Cf. *BN* 59; *EN* 70 on the explanatory contribution of an appeal to essence.
4. Cf., in this connection, his positive allusion to Husserl's eideitc reduction (*BN* 4; *EN* 14).
5. "… ne dépend pas de mon bon plaisir" (*EN* 13).
6. This is, I think, a more accurate rendering of Sartre's claim that "Tout est en act" (*EN* 12); Hazel Barnes translates this as "The act is everything" (*BN* 2).
7. My presentation of "being" as a twofold notion involving essence and existence is supported, among other things, by Sartre's interest in the fact that a phenomenal being "manifests its essence as well as its existence" (*BN* 3; *EN* 13).
8. As shown in Part III of *Being and Nothingness*, there is a further reason why substituting *being* with *presence* gives us the wrong account of the existence of entities in the Sartrean ontology. For Sartre, presence is a relational phenomenon, directed from a conscious being to its environing entities: we are present to someone or something; thus, properly speaking, it is not the cup, or the chest of drawers, that is present, but myself (as a conscious being) who is present to such (non-conscious) entities.
9. It might be useful to consider at this point a case described in the chapter on negation (*BN* pt I, ch. 1), where the object does "respond" to the enquirer: "If my car breaks down, it is the carburetor, or the spark-plugs, etc., that I question … What I expect from the carburetor … is not a judgment; it is a disclosure of being on the basis of which we can make a judgment" (*BN* 31). In contrast to that case where the interrogation targets the presence or absence of a particular property or capability of a thing, Sartre seems to be saying that interrogating an object regarding its being (understood either as its existence, or its essence) will not return any results.
10. Barnes's explication of "the question of the being-of-the-chair" as "the question of what it means to be a chair" retains an ambiguity that is absent from Heidegger's treatment of the question of the being of objects as pertaining primarily to their existing – to the fact that they are – and not to what they happen to be.
11. It appears to me that Sartre's remarks on this point are rather precipitate. An opponent might argue that being-as-revealed is different from being as the condition of revelation of beings. Thus, a grasp of being *as such* need not require a particular being whose being (i.e. whose existence) is to be revealed.
12. "Mode of being" translates two expressions that Sartre uses interchangeably: "*manière d'être*" (*EN* 15) and "*façon d'être*" (*EN* 24). Those phrases purport to convey Sartre's emphasis on the distinctive *manner*, *way* or *mode* in which something exists, and in the subsequent discussion I refer to all three notions, as required.
13. To the two modes, a third major mode is later introduced: that of "being-for-others" (*BN* pt III, esp. ch. 4).
14. Cf. "Consciousness has nothing substantial, it is pure 'appearance' in the sense that it exists only to the degree to which it appears to itself" (*BN* 12).
15. Cf. "The perceived thing is in front of consciousness; consciousness cannot reach it, and it can not enter into consciousness; and as the perceived being is cut off from consciousness, it exists cut off from its own existence" (*BN* 14).

16. In my view, some ways of debating that issue are more fruitful than others. See Gardner's (2009) important discussion on the "basic" and the "complete" ontology, as well as Webber's (2009) insightful remarks on the appropriate interpretation of some notorious phrases of that section, in light of Sartre's considered account of being-for-itself in *Being and Nothingness*, pt I, ch. 2.
17. "[M]ême à titre d'irréel, il faut bien qu'il existe" (*EN* 26). A translation closer to the letter of the text might be: "even under the heading of unreal, it should exist".
18. One might appreciate this basic point if one avoids confusing "existing" with other expressions that are used interchangeably in a colloquial context, although literally having a very different meaning, such as "conducting one's life", "growing up", "getting older" and so on, all of which might have *ways*, *manners* or *modes*.

Bibliography

Works by Sartre cited

1936. *L'Imagination*. Paris: Presses Universitaires de France.
1947. *Situations: Critiques littéraires*, vol. 1. Paris: Gallimard.
1960–85. *Critique de la raison dialectique*, vol. 1. Paris: Gallimard.
1970. "Intentionality: A Fundamental Idea in Husserl's Phenomenology", J. Fell (trans.). *Journal of the British Society of Phenomenology* 1(2): 4–5. Originally published as "Une Idée fondamentale de la phénoménologie de Husserl: L'intentionnalité", in *Situations I*, 31–4 (Paris: Gallimard, 1947).
1981a. *Oeuvres Romanesque*, M. Contat & M. Rybalka (eds). Paris: Gallimard, 1981.
1981b. "Saint Marc et son double", *Obliques* 24–5: 171–202. Reprinted in *Situations IV* (Paris: Gallimard, 1964).
1995. *Carnets de la drôle de guerre: Septembre 1939–Mars 1940*. Paris: Gallimard.
2000. *Nausea*, R. Baldick (trans.). Harmondsworth: Penguin. Originally published as *La Nausée* (Paris: Gallimard, 1938).
2003. *Being and Nothingness*, H. Barnes (trans.). London: Routledge. Originally published as *L'Être et le néant: Essai d'ontologie phénoménologique* (Paris: Gallimard, 1943 [rev. edn 1976]).
2004a. *The Imaginary: A Phenomenological Psychology of the Imagination*, J. Webber (trans.). London: Routledge. Originally published as *L'Imaginaire: Psychologie phénoménologique de l'imagination* (Paris: Gallimard, 1940).
2004b. *Sketch for a Theory of the Emotions*, P. Mariet (trans.). London: Routledge. Originally published as *Esquisse d'une théorie des émotions* (Paris: Hermann, 1939).
2004c. *The Transcendence of the Ego*, A. Brown (trans.). London: Routledge. Originally published in *Recherches Philosophiques* (1937); reprinted as *La Transcendance de l'Ego* (Paris: Vrin, 1988).

Other works

Bard, X. 2002. *Pour une lecture critique de la transcendance de l'ego: Contribution à l'examen des consciences non-thétiques*. Paris: L' Harmattan.
Barnes, H. 1959. *Humanistic Existentialism*. Lincoln, NE: University of Nebraska Press.

Barnes, H. 1967. *An Existentialist Ethics*. New York: Knopf.
Barnes, H. 1997. "Emotions in Sartre's Philosophy". In *Existentialist Ontology and Human Consciousness*, W. L. McBride (ed.). London: Routledge.
Block, N. 1983. "Mental Pictures and Cognitive Science". *Philosophical Review* **92**: 499–542.
Bolzano, B. 1837. *Wissenschaftslehre*. Sulzbach: J. E. v. Seidel.
Brandl, J. L. 2005. "The Immanence Theory of Intentionality". *In Phenomenology and Philosophy of Mind*, D. Woodruff Smith & A. L. Thomasson (eds), 167–82. Oxford: Oxford University Press.
Brentano, F. 1955. *Psychology from an Empirical Standpoint*, L. McAlister (trans.). New York: Humanities Press.
Cabestan, P. 2005. *Sartre: Désir et liberté*. Paris: Presses Universitaire de France.
Cannon, B. 1993. *Sartre et la Psychanalyse*. Paris: Presses Universitaire de France.
Carruthers, P. 2000. *Phenomenal Consciousness*. Cambridge: Cambridge University Press.
Casey, E. 2000. *Imagining: A Phenomenological Study*. Indianapolis, IN: Indiana University Press.
Contat, M. (ed.) 1996. *Pourquoi et comment Sartre a écrit Les Mots: Genèse d'une autobiographie*. Paris: Presses Universitaires de France.
Contat M. & M. Rybalka 1970. *Les Écrits de Sartre: Chronologie, bibliographie commenteé*. Paris: Gallimard.
Coorebyter, V. de 2000. *Sartre face à la phénoménologie*. Brussels: Ousia.
Crane, T. 2001. *Elements of Mind: An Introduction to the Philosophy of Mind*. Oxford: Oxford University Press.
Crane, T. 2003. "The Intentional Structure of Consciousness". In *Consciousness: New Philosophical Perspectives,* A. Jokic & Q. Smith (eds), 33–56. Oxford: Oxford University Press.
D'Arms, J. & D. Jacobson 2003. "The Significance of Recalcitrant Emotion (or, Anti-quasi-judgmentalism)". In *Philosophy and the Emotions*, A. Hatzimoysis (ed.), 163–80. Cambridge: Cambridge University Press.
Damasio, A. 1999. *The Feeling of What Happens: Body, Emotion and the Making of Consciousness*. London: Vintage.
Dancy, J. 1993. *Moral Reasons*. Oxford: Blackwell.
Darwall, S., A. Gibbard & P. A. Railton (eds) 1997. *Moral Discourse and Practice: Some Philosophical Approaches*. Oxford: Oxford University Press.
Deigh, J. 1996. *The Sources of Moral Agency: Essays In Moral Psychology and Freudian Theory*. Cambridge: Cambridge University Press.
DeLancey, C. 2002. *Passionate Engines: What Emotions Reveal about the Mind and Artificial Intelligence*. New York: Oxford University Press.
Döring, S. 2003. "Explaining Action by Emotion". *Philosophical Quarterly* **211**: 214–30.
Dreyfus, H. L. & M. A. Wrathal (eds) 2006. *A Companion to Phenomenology and Existentialism*. Oxford: Blackwell.
Drummond, J. J. 2003. "The Structure of Intentionality". In *The New Husserl: A Critical Reader*, D. Welton (ed.), 65–92. Indianapolis, IN: Indiana University Press.
Edwards, M. 1971. "*La Nausée* – A Symbolist Novel". *Adam* **35**(343–5) (1970): 9–21.
Ekman, P. 1980. "Biological and Cultural Contributions to Body and Facial Movement in the Expression of Emotions". In *Explaining Emotions*, A. O. Rorty (ed.), 73–102. Berkeley, CA: University of California Press.
Esteves, F., U. Dimberg & A. Öhman 1994. "Automatically Elicited Fear: Conditioned

Skin Conductance Responses to Masked Facial Expressions". *Cognition and Emotion* **8**: 393–413.

Fish, W. 2010. *Philosophy of Perception: A Contemporary Introduction*. London: Routledge.

Fletcher, D. 1968. "The Use of Colour in *La Nausée*". *Modern Language Review* **63**: 370–80.

Freud, S. 1953–74. *The Standard Edition of the Complete Psychological Works of Sigmund Freud*, 24 vols. London: Hogarth Press.

Gardner, S. 2009. *Sartre's Being and Nothingness*. London: Continuum.

Gennaro, R. 2002. "Jean-Paul Sartre and the HOT Theory of Consciousness". *Canadian Journal of Philosophy* **32**: 293–330.

Goldie, P. 2000. *The Emotions: A Philosophical Exploration*. Oxford: Clarendon Press.

Goldthorpe, R. 1968. "The Presentation of Consciousness in Sartre's *La Nauseé* and its Theoretical Basis: 1. Reflection and Facticity". *French Studies* **22**: 114–32.

Griffiths, P. E. 1997. *What Emotions Really Are: The Problem of Psychological Categories*. Chicago, IL: University of Chicago Press.

Griffiths, P. E. 2003. "Basic Emotions, Complex Emotions, Machiavellian Emotions". In *Philosophy and the Emotions*, A. Hatzimoysis (ed.), 39–67. Cambridge: Cambridge University Press.

Hatzimoysis, A. 2003a. "The Philosopher and his Novel". *Philosophical Inquiry* **25**: 124–35.

Hatzimoysis, A. 2003b. "Emotional Feelings and Intentionalism". In *Philosophy and the Emotions*, A. Hatzimoysis (ed.), 105–12. Cambridge: Cambridge University Press.

Hatzimoysis, A. 2003c. "Sentimental Value". *Philosophical Quarterly* **53**(212): 373–9.

Hatzimoysis, A. (ed.) 2003d. *Philosophy and the Emotions*. Cambridge: Cambridge University Press.

Hatzimoysis, A. 2007. "The Case Against Unconscious Emotions". *Analysis* **64**(4): 292–9.

Hatzimoysis, A. 2010a. "Emotions in Heidegger and Sartre". In *The Oxford Handbook of Philosophy of Emotion*, P. Goldie (ed.), 215–36. Oxford: Oxford University Press.

Hatzimoysis, A. 2010b. "A Sartrean Critique of Introspection". In *Reading Sartre*, Jonathan Webber (ed.), 90–99. London: Routledge.

Hatzimoysis, A. 2011. "Introduction". In *Self-Knowledge*, A. Hatzimoysis (ed.), 1–8. Oxford: Oxford University Press.

Heidegger, M. 1962. *Being and Time*, J. Macquarrie & E. Robinson (trans.). Oxford: Blackwell.

Helm, B. W. 2010. "Emotion and Motivation: Reconsidering the Neo-Jamesian Accounts". In *The Oxford Handbook of Philosophy of Emotion*, P. Goldie (ed.), 303–24. Oxford: Oxford University Press.

Hopkins, R. 1998. *Picture, Image, and Experience*. Cambridge: Cambridge University Press.

Howells, C. (ed.) 1992. *The Cambridge Companion to Sartre*. Cambridge: Cambridge University Press.

Hurley, S. & A. Noë 2003. "Neural Plasticity and Consciousness". *Biology and Philosophy* **18**: 131–68.

Hursthouse, R. 1991. "Arational Actions". *Journal of Philosophy* **88**: 57–68.

Husserl, E. 1913. *Ideas Pertaining to a Pure Phenomenology and to a Phenomenological*

Philosophy, First Book: General Introduction to a Pure Phenomenology, F. Kersten (trans.). The Hague: Nijhoff.
Janet, P. 1909. *Les Névroses*. Paris: Flammarion.
Janet, P. 1927. *La Pensée Intérieure et Ses Troubles*. Paris: Chanine-Maloine.
Kearney, R. 1998. *Poetics of Imagining*. Edinburgh: Edinburgh University Press.
Kelly, S. D. 2003. "Edmund Husserl and Phenomenology". In *Blackwell Guide to Continental Philosophy*, R. Solomon & D. L. Sherman (eds), 112–42. Oxford: Blackwell.
Kriegel, U. 2003. "Consciousness as Intransitive Self-Consciousness: Two Views and an Argument". *Canadian Journal of Philosophy* **33**: 103–32.
Lacewing, M. 2007. "Do Unconscious Emotions Involve Unconscious Feelings?" *Philosophical Psychology* **20**: 81–104.
Lane, R. D., L. Sechrest, R. Reidel, V. Weldon, A. Kaszniak & G. E. Schwartz 1996. "Impaired Verbal and Nonverbal Emotion Recognition in Alexithymia". *Psychosomatic Medicine* **58**: 203–10.
Lane, R. D., G. L. Ahern, G. E. Schwartz & A. Kaszniak 1997. "Is Alexithymia the Emotional Equivalent of Blindsight?" *Biological Psychiatry* **42**: 834–44.
Lear, J. 2005. *Freud*. London: Routledge.
LeDoux, J. E. 1984. "Cognition and Emotion: Processing Functions and Brain Systems". In *Handbook of Cognitive Neuroscience*, M. Gazzaniga (ed.), 357–68. New York: Plenum.
Lormand, E. 2006. "Phenomenal Impressions". In *Perceptual Experience*, T. Szabo Gendler & J. Hawthorne (eds), 316–53. Oxford: Clarendon Press.
Marbach, E. 1993. *Mental Representation and Consciousness: Towards A Phenomenological Theory of Representation and Reference*. Dordrecht: Kluwer.
Martin, M. G. F. 1992. "Sight and Touch". In *The Contents of Experience: Essays on Perception*, T. Crane (ed.), 196–215. Cambridge: Cambridge University Press.
McCulloch, G. 1994. *Using Sartre: An Analytical Introduction to Early Sartrean Themes*. London: Routledge.
Merleau-Ponty M. [1945] 1962. *Phenomenology of Perception*, C. Smith (trans.). New York: Routledge & Kegan Paul.
Moore, G. E. 1966. "The Refutation of Idealism". In *Twentieth Century Philosophy: The Analytic Tradition*, M. Weitz (ed.), 15–34. New York: Free Press.
Morris, K. 2008. *Sartre*. Oxford: Blackwell.
Morris, P. S. 1985. "Sartre on the Transcendence of the Ego". *Philosophy and Phenomenological Research* **46**(2): 179–98.
Murdoch, I. 1953. *Sartre: Romantic Rationalist*. New Haven, CT: Yale University Press.
Murphy, J. S. (ed.) 1999. *Feminist Interpretations of Jean-Paul Sartre*. University Park, PA: Pennsylvania State University Press.
Neu, J. 2000. *A Tear is an Intellectual Thing: The Meanings of Emotion*. New York: Oxford University Press.
Nudds, M. 2001. "Experiencing the Production of Sounds". *European Journal of Philosophy* **9**(2): 210–29.
Nussbaum, M. 2001. *Upheavals of Thought: The Intelligence of Emotions*. Cambridge: Cambridge University Press.
O'Shaughnessy, B. 2002. *Consciousness and the World*. Oxford: Clarendon Press.
Öhman, A. & J. Soares 1994. "Unconscious Anxiety: Phobic Responses to Masked Stimuli". *Journal of Abnormal Psychology* **103**: 231–40.
Peacocke, C. 1998. "Conscious Attitudes, Attention and Self-Knowledge". In

Knowing Our Own Minds, C. Wright, B. Smith & C. MacDonald (eds), 63–98. Oxford: Oxford University Press.

Pickard, H. 2003. "Emotions and the Problem of Other Minds". In *Philosophy and the Emotions*, A. Hatzimoysis (ed.), 87–104. Cambridge: Cambridge University Press.

Priest, S. 2000. *The Subject in Question*. London: Routledge.

Prinz, J. 2004. *Gut Reactions: A Perceptual Theory of Emotion*. New York: Oxford University Press.

Ribot, T. 1896. *La Psychologie des sentiments*. Paris: Felix Alcan.

Richmond, S. 2007. "Sartre and Bergson: A Disagreement about Nothingness". *International Journal of Philosophical Studies* **15**(1): 77–95.

Richmond, S. 2010. "Magic in Sartre's Early Philosophy". In *Reading Sartre*, J. Webber (ed.), 145–61. London: Routledge.

Sayre-McCord, G. 1988. *Essays on Moral Realism*. Ithaca, NY: Cornell University Press.

Schroeder, W. R. 2004. "Jean-Paul Sartre: *Being and Nothingness*". In *Central Works of Philosophy*, vol. 4, J. Shand (ed.), 155–76. Chesham: Acumen.

Searle, J. 1992. *The Rediscovery of the Mind*. Cambridge, MA: MIT Press.

Sifneos, P. E. 1972. *Short-term Psychotherapy and Emotional Crisis*. Cambridge, MA: Harvard University Press.

Smith, M. 1998. "The Possibility of Action". In *Human Action*, J. Bransen (ed.), 17–41. Dordrecht: Kluwer.

Sokolowski, R.2000. *Introduction to Phenomenology*. Cambridge: Cambridge University Press.

Solomon, R. 2003. "Emotions, Thoughts and Feelings: What is a 'Cognitive Theory' of the Emotions and Does It Neglect Affectivity?" In *Philosophy and the Emotions*, A. Hatzimoysis (ed.), 1–18. Cambridge: Cambridge University Press.

Solomon, R. 2004. *In Defense of Sentimentality*. Oxford: Oxford University Press.

Spanos, W. 1978. "The Un-Naming of the Beasts: the Postmodernity of Sartre's La Nausée". *Criticism* **20**: 223–80.

Stawarska, B. 2005. "Defining Imagination: Sartre between Husserl and Janet". *Phenomenology and the Cognitive Sciences* **4** (2): 133–53.

Stephen P. 2000 *The Subject in Question. Sartre's Critique of Husserl in the Transcendence of the Ego*. London: Routledge.

Tappolet, C. 2010. "Emotion, Motivation, and Action: the Case of Fear". In *The Oxford Handbook of Philosophy of Emotion*, P. Goldie (ed.), 325–45. Oxford: Oxford University Press.

Tye, M. 1995. *Ten Problems of Consciousness*. Cambridge, MA: MIT Press.

Warnock, M. 1970 "Imagination in Sartre". *British Journal of Aesthetics* **10**(4): 323–36.

Webber, J. 2009. *The Existentialism of Jean-Paul Sartre*. New York: Routledge.

Webber, J. (ed.) 2010. *Reading Sartre on Phenomenology and Existentialism*. London: Routledge.

Wider, K. 1997. *The Bodily Nature of Consciousness*. Ithaca, NY: Cornell University Press.

Wilford, K. 2006. "The Self-Representational Structure of Consciousness". In *Self-Representational Approaches to Consciousness*, U. Kriegel & K. Wilford (eds). Cambridge, MA: MIT Press.

Wollheim, R. 1991. *Freud*. London: Fontana.

Wood, J. 2000. "Editor's Introduction". In *Nausea*, J-P. Sartre, vii–xx. Harmondsworth: Penguin.

Zahavi, D. 2003. *Husserl's Phenomenology*. Stanford, CA: Stanford University Press.
Zajonc, R. 1984. "On the Primacy of Affect". *American Psychologist* **39**: 117–23.
Zajonc, R., S. Murphy & M. Inglehart 1989. "Feeling and Facial Efference: Implications of the Vascular Theory of Emotion". *Psychological Review* **96**: 395–416.

Index